YANKED INTO ETERNITY

Lynchings and Hangings in Missouri

~~~~~~~~

Larry Wood

Hickory Press
Joplin, Missouri

ISBN: 9780970282989

LCCN: 2017900513

Published by
    Hickory Press
    Joplin, MO

Table of Contents

Preface

The word "lynch" originally referred to any extralegal punishment, and "lynching" did not routinely result in death. The most accepted theory of the word's derivation traces it to Charles Lynch, a county judge in Virginia during the Revolutionary War era who often exceeded his jurisdiction, dispensing his own brand of justice, known as "Lynch law." Over the years, the word "lynch" came to be applied almost exclusively to those cases in which the victim of the vigilante punishment died. Nowadays, "lynching" is often associated specifically with extralegal hanging by a mob. I have, with just one or two exceptions, adopted this narrow meaning of "lynch" for the purposes of this book, and all the legal executions that I examine in the book are also hangings. In short, this book is mainly about Missouri hangings, legal and otherwise.

It is not an attempt to duplicate the effort of Harriett Frazier, whose books *Death Sentences in Missouri, 1803-2005* and *Lynchings in Missouri, 1803-1981* remain the definitive works about legal and extralegal executions in the state. Professor Frazier's books contain appendices listing every instance of lynching and every instance of legal execution in Missouri history that she was able to confirm, and her approach in the text itself is also comprehensive. Her books cover the breadth of legal and illegal executions in the state and examine them and their social ramifications in historical context. Because of their comprehensive nature, her books generally chronicle individual instances of lynchings and legal executions only in brief fashion within the context of a broader discussion.

This book, on the other hand, covers a relatively small number of the many lynchings and legal hangings that have occurred in Missouri history, but it covers those few and the stories behind them in some detail. To succinctly state the difference between Frazier's books and this one, hers are about the overall subject of legal and extralegal execution in Missouri, while mine is about a few of the state's individual hangings and lynchings.

Several criteria influenced which stories I chose to chronicle in this book.

First and foremost, in order for a lynching or hanging to be included, sufficient details about it had to be available in contemporaneous newspapers and other sources to tell the story in somewhat complete fashion. There have been hundreds of lynchings and hangings in Missouri history, but the stories behind many of them have been lost to time because of a lack of documentation. The details of many of the lynchings were never written down to begin with because they often happened in secrecy and were, therefore, known to few people. In many other cases, including the legal hangings, whatever written sources that might have once existed have been destroyed in fires and other disasters or simply lost.

Another criterion for an incident's inclusion in this book was that the hanging or lynching had to be one that I had not previously chronicled in one of my other books. This excluded a number of infamous incidents in Missouri, especially the Ozarks, that resulted in lynching or hanging, such as the murder of the Parsons family and the hanging of Jodie Hamilton in Texas County, which I wrote about in *Desperadoes of the Ozarks*. I have also excluded a few very notorious Missouri lynchings that other authors have already chronicled extensively, such as the lynching of Raymond Gunn in 1931 at Maryville and the lynching of Cleo Wright in 1942 at Sikeston, each of which has been the subject of at least one entire book.

In addition, I have tried to balance the number of lynchings of black men and white men I chronicled to roughly reflect the proportion that actually exists in the history of Missouri, although most of the black lynchings I have included were bunched in a relatively short period of time around the turn of the twentieth century during America's so-called "lynching era." I did not make a proportional effort in selecting the legal hangings that I chronicled. I just picked the ones that struck me as interesting and about which sufficient information existed.

Acknowledgements

The fact that newspapers and other documents, like census records, are increasingly available online nowadays has facilitated modern-day historical research so that a lot of it can be done from one's home computer. Therefore, I do not seem to have as many people to thank as I have had with some of my past projects.

However, a lot of newspapers, books, and other records are still available only in print or on microfilm; and the Joplin Public Library continues to be my home base for hands-on research. I especially want to thank reference librarians Patty Crane and Jason Sullivan for fulfilling my many interlibrary loan requests.

I also wish to thank Cheyenne Flotree, director of the Jasper County Records Center, for his help with my research on the Worden brothers and for supplying a photograph of Lew Worden.

I want to express my appreciation to Maryville historian Letha Mowry for answering several questions on local history for me during my research on Omaha Charley.

Finally, I thank my wife, Gigi, for her proofreading skills and for her continued support of my writing efforts.

1

An Unnatural and Atrocious Crime

Stephens Family Murder and Hanging of John Duncan

On December 13, 1820, twenty-year-old John Duncan called at the home of John B. Stephens two and a half miles east of Fredericktown in Madison County, Missouri, representing himself as a prospective land buyer. After visiting at the house for a short while, Stephens asked Duncan whether he was ready to look at the land, and Duncan said he was. Stephens took hold of Duncan's gun, suggesting that he leave it in the house and retrieve it after they returned, but Duncan said, "No, we might see something to shoot." What Stephens didn't know was that Duncan already had a target in mind, because he hadn't come to look at Stephens's land.

He'd come to kill him.

All the way from Sumner County, Tennessee.

At the first term of the Madison County Circuit Court in July 1819, an indictment for larceny had been brought against John B. Stephens, accused of stealing a considerable sum of money from his neighbor David L. Caruthers. There was insufficient evidence to convict him, but bad blood lingered between Caruthers and Stephens. Caruthers began plotting with his friends Samuel and William Anthony on how to retrieve the money he felt sure Stephens had stolen from him. Like Duncan, the Anthony brothers were originally from Sumner County, and Samuel Anthony summoned the young man to Missouri to help deal with the Stephens matter.

Duncan arrived in Madison County from Tennessee in late September, 1820, and boarded at first with Samuel

Anthony. About a week after his arrival, Anthony detailed to him the situation with John B. Stephens. Anthony said that he and others had tried various ways to get Stephens to confess to stealing Caruthers's money, including one time when they had flogged him mercilessly, giving him about 300 lashes. Duncan replied that he thought flogging was the wrong way to go about extracting a confession because, after a certain number of lashes, the person became numb to the pain. If he was doing it, Duncan added, he would either build a fire and hold Stephens's bare feet to the flame or else dig a grave and take him to it with the threat of burying him alive. Anthony replied that the latter idea seemed like a good plan and that he knew another man, George Nifong, who could help Duncan carry it out. Duncan assured Anthony that if he and the others would get Stephens out into the woods, he (Duncan) could make him confess to stealing Caruthers's money.

A few days later, Duncan met with Nifong to discuss his plan, and later the same day he went to stay with David Caruthers. He was already there when Caruthers came home carrying a spade. Duncan asked him what he was doing with a spade, and Caruthers said he was going to dig a grave. Duncan then asked whether Caruthers had heard about his plan for making Stephens confess, and Caruthers made no reply. Later Nifong showed up, but he backed out of the scheme, saying that he was already involved in one difficulty and couldn't afford to get involved in another one.

After Nifong left, Duncan, speaking of Stephens, offered flatly to "put him out of the way" if Caruthers would give him "something handsome." Caruthers replied that he dared not, solely on his own, hire Duncan or anyone else to murder Stephens but he was sure that, if Duncan or some other person were to put Stephens out of the way, he (Caruthers) and the other "regulators" in the area would be able come up with "a handsome sum" for such a person to help him get out of the territory. Caruthers added that, if he didn't have a family, he would put Stephens out of the way himself and then slip out of the region. He was sure no one would follow him or anybody else who might do the deed. Stephens was so generally disliked, Caruthers said, that he doubted whether Stephens's own brother would try to track down such a person.

Duncan stayed with Caruthers about six weeks and then moved to William Anthony's house for a few days. He continued over the next few weeks to make his home alternately with Caruthers and the Anthony brothers, and as he moved from place to place, the three men continued discussing plans for dealing with Stephens. According to Duncan's later statement, Caruthers and Samuel Anthony kept insisting on him "taking Stephens out," and by mid-December, Duncan had let himself be persuaded.

With an apparent stamp of approval from Caruthers and Samuel Anthony, Duncan had now arrived at Stephens's place to "put him out of the way." As he lured Stephens from the house under the guise of inspecting his land, Stephens's little boy and a couple of dogs trailed behind them. They had gone but a short distance when the dogs chased a rabbit into a hollow tree. Duncan was having second thoughts about carrying out his murderous scheme, but as Stephens started cutting out the hole in the tree so he could twist the rabbit out, Duncan decided once again to kill the man. Stepping back about ten feet, he cocked his gun, but again his resolve weakened and he couldn't pull the trigger.

Stephens stopped up the hole in the tree to trap the rabbit inside and sent his son back to the house to fetch an ax. After the boy left, Duncan and Stephens again started off together to look at the land, with Stephens leading the way and Duncan trailing behind. After walking some distance in this manner, Duncan raised his gun and shot Stephens in the back. Stephens cried out "Oh, Lord!" and fell to the ground. Stepping up to Stephens, Duncan replied with an oath that he'd come 300 miles for the express purpose of killing him, and he then struck him with the barrel of his gun. Putting his own gun aside, he picked up Stephens's gun and struck the fallen man several more times with it. Finally Duncan took out a knife and cut the man's throat.

After killing Stephens, Duncan went to a creek and washed the blood off himself. Realizing that the man's wife and kids still stood in the way of his getting the large sum of money ($1,500 or $1,600) that Caruthers had led him to believe Stephens had, Duncan decided to kill the rest of the family, too. He reloaded his gun and started toward the house. On the way, he met the boy returning with the ax. Taking the ax, he accompanied the boy to the tree where the rabbit was. After they unstopped the hole, Duncan asked the lad to look into it. As soon as the boy leaned over to look in the hole, Duncan struck him on the side of the head with the ax and followed up with several more blows, making sure he was dead.

The murderer then went to the house and told Mrs. Stephens her husband needed her to help identify a certain corner of their land. The woman immediately started away with Duncan followed by her youngest child, a little boy, leaving her two daughters to mind the house. They had gone some distance from the house when Duncan tried several times to shoot the woman, but the gun kept misfiring. Hearing the snapping, Mrs. Stephens turned and said, "Oh, Duncan, don't do that!" The killer promptly knocked her down with the gun and sliced her throat, according to Duncan's own subsequent statement, but a *St. Louis Missouri Gazette and Public Advertiser* account claimed "the inhuman butcher insulted her and abused her body in a most shocking manner" before killing her.

Duncan then caught the young boy and cut his throat as well. Or, in the words of the contemporaneous *Gazette* report, "To cap the climax of his infamy and barbarity, he severed the head from the body of the infant."

Returning to the creek, Duncan again washed his hands and then started to the house with the intent of killing the Stephens girls. On the way, he met Warren Stephens, another son, and thought about killing him, too, but decided to let him pass. When Duncan got to the house, he was met by the youngest girl, but, instead of killing her, he told her that her father had sent him to fetch all of his money and take it to him. Duncan and the girl searched through a chest and found $68, which he carried off as his "dear-earned booty" for killing four people.

Word of the murders quickly spread, and Duncan was pursued by a posse and captured within a day or two. He was lodged in the Madison County Jail at Fredericktown to await "the vengeance of the law as the just retribution of Heaven for his unnatural and atrocious crimes."

FROM THE MISSOURIAN.

MOST HORRID MURDER!

On the 13th inst. John B. Duncan a-ged 19 years, went to the house of John B Stephens, in the county of Madison, (Missouri) with the pretence of purchasing his tract of land, and induced Stephens to go with him to examine. After decoy-

Duncan's crime made headlines across the U.S. *From the Poughkeepsie (NY) Journal.*

Duncan was tried in early 1821, found guilty, and sentenced to hang on April 5. He had confessed shortly after his capture, and he made it official on April 4, the day before his scheduled execution, by giving a full written statement. (It's not entirely clear whether he wrote the confession himself or it was transcribed by someone else.)

In the days leading up to the execution, a scaffold was erected near Saline Creek in the northeast part of Fredericktown at a place that came to be known as "Duncan's Hole." On April 5, several hundred people poured into town from all parts of Madison and surrounding counties to witness the hanging. Based on Duncan's confession,

Samuel Anthony and Caruthers had been indicted as accomplices to the murder of the Stephens family, but the condemned man amended his confession on the scaffold, taking full blame for the decision to commit the murders and, thus, exonerating Anthony and Caruthers.

2

An Election Day Mob

The Lynching of Abraham W. Smith

William Vincent of Madison County, Missouri, fell
sick in December of 1843, and after his condition took a turn
for the worse, his brother Thomas and neighbor Abraham W.
Smith sat up with him at his home on the night of December
27. About midnight, Thomas Vincent left to go to his own
home, explaining that he planned to ride to Fredericktown
early the next morning to summon a doctor and that he
needed to get a few hours' rest.

Meanwhile, Smith stayed with the patient.

But not all night.

Early the next morning he lay in ambush in a thicket
at the crossing of Trace Creek south of Fredericktown where
he knew Thomas Vincent would have to pass on his way to
town. As Vincent stopped at the creek to water his horse,
Smith raised up and shot him in the chest just below the
heart.

Gravely wounded but still in the saddle, Vincent
exclaimed, "Why Smith, you have shot me!" He then
wheeled his horse around, rode back to the home of Michael
Shetley, and asked Shetley to notify his family that he'd been
shot. Vincent lingered about eight hours and gave an account
of the shooting before he died that was taken down by a
justice of the peace.

The motive for Smith's crime is not altogether clear.
According to local lore, Smith and Vincent had previously
argued over Vincent's livestock getting into Smith's
cornfield. However, when this dispute occurred and,
therefore, whether it was the immediate provocation for the

crime is unknown. The Vincent family alleged also that Smith was prone to violence and had previously killed a man, and Goodspeed's 1888 *History of Southeast Missouri* said he had "borne a bad reputation" prior to the Vincent murder.

In an ironic and tragic twist to the story, William Vincent died on the same day his brother was killed, and they were buried together.

Immediately after the murder, Smith walked to the home of a man named Duncan, about two miles away, and told Duncan what he had done. Duncan told Smith he'd "better be drinking 'Orleans water,'" meaning he needed to take off for New Orleans or some other faraway place.

Before he could flee, though, Smith was captured by Dempsey Odem and his son, Marshall Odem, who were Thomas Vincent's father-in-law and brother-in-law. The two men held Smith until authorities arrived to take charge of him and lodge him in the Madison County Jail at Fredericktown.

Smith was indicted for first degree murder and tried at the April 1844 term of the Madison County Circuit Court. He was convicted of first degree murder, based largely on Vincent's dying statement, and sentenced to be hanged by the neck on June 1, 1844, "until he be dead, dead, dead." Smith's motion for a new trial was overruled, but his appeal to the Missouri Supreme Court was allowed and the execution postponed pending the outcome of the appeal.

On Saturday, June 1, the originally scheduled day for the hanging, a large crowd, estimated at close to a thousand people, gathered in Fredericktown, and there was much talk of lynching Smith. A small mob organized for that purpose, but, according to the *St. Louis Daily Missouri Republican*, it "was opposed by upwards of three-fourths of the people assembled, who succeeded on that day in dispersing those whose wish was to violate the law."

After the foiled attempt to lynch Smith, he was moved to the Cape Girardeau County Jail at Jackson for safe-keeping. Sometime after June 1, the Supreme Court sustained the verdict against Smith and reset his execution for

September 1. In July, Smith was brought back to Fredericktown for another hearing. The nature of the hearing is not known, but it might have pertained to an attempt on the part of Smith's lawyer to obtain another delay in the sentence.

At any rate, on Monday, August 5, which was Election Day, a large crowd once again assembled in Fredericktown. In nineteen-century America, Election Day was often a day for revelry and drinking, and this day in Fredericktown was no exception. In due course, a mob of about fourteen or fifteen drunken men organized and marched on the jail. When their demand that the sheriff turn over the keys was refused, they overpowered the lawman, went to work with crow-bars and axes, and soon "shattered the doors of the jail to atoms," said the *Daily Missouri Republican*.

After the mob broke into the jail, one of the gang got down in the dungeon-like cell, where the prisoner was held in irons, and placed a rope around Smith's neck. The rest of the mob hauled him up by the rope and then literally dragged him down some stairs and outside.

According to the St. Louis newspaper, the mob found very few among the large crowd "willing to aid or assist them," but they apparently found very few as well who were willing to actively oppose them. After they dragged Smith from his cell, according to Vincent family lore, the leader of the mob addressed the large crowd, calling for all those in favor of hanging Smith to step to the right side and all those opposed to step to the left side. The whole crowd supposedly moved to the right side, as Smith, "a coward at heart," kept yelling "murder" and begging pathetically for his life. Thomas Vincent's widow, Hannah, was among the gathered crowd, and she was asked whether she desired Smith to hang. She replied that she could forgive the prisoner for killing her husband but that she was afraid that, if he were to go free, he would return and kill her and her kids as he had reportedly threatened to do. This clinched the verdict, and the crowd was more determined than ever to see Smith strung up.

Goodspeed's history adds credence to the idea that a vote on whether Smith should hang might have been taken among the crowd, or at least proposed. According to the local history, the sheriff himself suggested such a vote, as a way of thwarting the mob's intent, after he and his deputies had held off the vigilantes for almost two hours, because he felt sure a majority of those present would vote to uphold the law. As soon as this was agreed to, however, the deputies left, and the mob made its dash on the jail.

Having dragged the prisoner from his cell, the mob now took him to a walnut tree located about fifty yards from the jail. Here they compelled a Methodist minister to say a prayer for the condemned man.

Notwithstanding the fact that Smith was apparently already dead from being dragged by the neck, they strung him up to the tree and let him hang for several minutes. They then let him down, but one of the gang, suspecting Smith might still be alive, insisted that they hang him again. The body was accordingly strung back up until the bloodthirsty mob was sufficiently convinced that life was extinct.

That very night, an inquest was held over Smith's body, and the jury returned a verdict that he had come to his death at the hands of a mob that included Jones, Sinclair, Mayse, Pollis, Cox, Blackburn, Shetley, and five other men. Pollis, Cox, Blackburn, Shetley and one other man suspected in the vigilante execution were promptly arrested. Several days later Mayse was spotted at St. Mary's Landing, a small community on the Mississippi River in Ste. Genevieve County. It was presumed he was trying to catch a boat to make his escape. Around the first of October, John Sinclair was recognized on the streets of St. Louis and arrested. Accused of being the man who had placed the rope around Smith's neck, he was taken back to Madison County, where he and thirteen other men involved in the lynching of Smith were indicted on charges of murder. Most of the gang members died, however, within a year or so, before they could come to trial, and none of them were ever convicted.

3

A Terrible Murder

Lynchings of Jeff Kessler and James Milligan

Samuel Timmons was a Bogle Township constable charged with enforcing the law in the north-central part of Gentry County, Missouri, when he got into a minor scrape with the law himself in early June of 1858. After hearing the complaint against Timmons, D. P. Gregg, a justice of the township, swore out a warrant for Timmons's arrest and placed it in the hands of constable pro tem Jeff Kessler.

Near the middle of June, Kessler, taking nineteen-year-old James Milligan along with him as a deputy, went out to Timmons's farm near the Worth County border to make the arrest. Previous bad blood existed between Timmons and Kessler, and Timmons, having gotten word of his imminent arrest, had left his house to avoid Kessler and was not there when the two men arrived. Leaving Milligan at the house, Kessler went looking for Timmons and located him elsewhere on the property.

In the confrontation that followed, Kessler shot and killed Timmons. According to the 1882 *History of Gentry and Worth Counties*, Kessler shot Timmons in the back with a shotgun and left the body lying in the field. Returning to the house to pick up his deputy, Kessler rode away without even bothering to inform the dead man's wife of the shooting. Late that night, she discovered her husband dead, apparently having been shot in the back.

The county historian added that Timmons was considered a good citizen, while Kessler was known as "a man of bad character" who had committed other desperate deeds. Contemporaneous newspaper accounts confirm that the circumstances of the killing, whatever their exact nature might have been, "made the act in the estimation of the people a cruel injustice."

Several recent murders and other crimes had occurred in northern Gentry and southern Worth counties, and the perpetrators had gone unpunished. In response, a group of men, primarily citizens of Worth County, met at Oxford and adopted a plan to put a stop to the outbreak of crime. They resolved that there should be no delays in meting out justice to lawbreakers and that, if the courts failed to vigorously prosecute the criminals, the citizens would take the law into their own hands.

Jeff Kessler was about to be their first example.

He and Milligan were arrested on a warrant issued by Bogle Township justice Henry Carlock, and when they were brought before him on June 18, a large crowd, mostly men who had attended the Oxford meeting, gathered with the idea of lynching the prisoners immediately. The would-be vigilantes were deterred from mob action only on the condition that circuit judge E. H. Norton be summoned at once to conduct a trial. They also demanded that no continuances or changes of venue be granted, although Carlock, of course, had no power to determine that. The crowd reportedly took a vote on whether to hang the defendants on the spot, and even with the assurances of a speedy trial, the motion failed by only three or four votes.

Kessler and Milligan waived examination before Justice Carlock, and they were taken to Albany, the seat of Gentry County, to await trial. They were held under a close guard at the courthouse, since the county had no jail at the time. A runner was sent to Platte City, headquarters of the circuit court district, to inform Judge Norton of the exigent circumstances in the Timmons murder case. Norton left Platte City on June 22, and, arriving in Albany, called a special session of the circuit court for the 24th. On the first day, a grand jury returned a true bill charging Kessler and Milligan with murder in the first degree. In response to the whisperings of a lynching, Judge Norton ordered the sheriff to gather a posse of twenty-five trusted men to help guard the prisoners until their cases were settled.

The trial began the next day, June 25, before a large crowd. Kessler's and Milligan's cases were severed, and both pleaded not guilty. Their attorney then asked for and was granted a recess until 1:00 p.m. to decide his strategy. The lawyer came back at that hour and told the judge that the main two defense witnesses had been driven off and could not be located. He asked that Kessler's trial be continued at the regular session of court later in the year, and Judge Norton granted the delay. He then granted a continuance in Milligan's case as well and adjourned the court.

The judge and the attorneys slipped out through a window as the crowd of six or seven hundred spectators filed out of the courtroom. About twenty or thirty men lagged behind, though, and as soon as the room was nearly clear, they made a rush toward the prisoners. All the deputies who were helping guard the prisoners, except three or four, deserted the sheriff at the first sign of trouble. Colonel John Scott went to the sheriff's assistance, however, and the officers had almost succeeded in securing the prisoners when a horde of men at least as large as the first group burst into the courtroom from outside to augment their fellow vigilantes.

The mob, now numbering from 50 to 100, quickly wrested Kessler from the sheriff and his small posse, although Milligan was spirited away to an upstairs room and was not pursued. The vigilantes dragged Kessler from the courthouse amid the screams and pleas of his wife and three children.

The prisoner was taken to the edge of a woods about 150 yards from the courthouse. He was halted beneath an elm tree in full view of the town, and a rope, such as was commonly used for bed cords at the time, was placed around his neck. He requested that he be allowed to make out a will, and a lawyer was summoned for that purpose. He was then blindfolded with a handkerchief tied over his eyes, and a preacher was exhorted to offer a final prayer for the condemned man. Kessler prayed, too, and he begged to see his wife and kids before he was lynched. The handkerchief was removed so as to grant the request, but an old man among the mob sneered that Kessler hadn't given Timmons the same courtesy.

At this point, two citizens intervened with earnest speeches entreating the mob to let the law take its course, but the same old man replied, "He that sheddeth man's blood, by man shall his blood be shed." So, the rope was promptly thrown over a limb of the elm, and Kessler was positioned beneath it. Three men tried to draw him up but were not strong enough, and the leader of the mob ordered more men to the task. With two yanks, the vigilantes then pulled Kessler up about three feet before the rope broke and he fell to the ground. He was lifted back up, the rope was speedily retied, and, in the words of the *St. Joseph Journal*, "the spirit of the unfortunate man was launched into eternity."

In the wake of the lynching, a correspondent to the *St. Louis Republican* called the mob action a "terrible murder." Kessler had declared until the very last that he was not guilty. He said he had only gone to Timmons's place because he'd been ordered to make an arrest and that he had fired in self-defense when Timmons drew a gun on him. The same writer claimed that, although Jim Milligan was allowed to live, many people felt his execution would have been more excusable than Kessler's because Milligan had been suspected of having shot the sheriff some time earlier.

The correspondent had no way of knowing it, but Milligan's time was coming.

After Kessler was hanged, Milligan was carefully watched at the courthouse by citizens who received no compensation for their guard duty. Some of them became "wearied with so thankless and tedious an employment and abandoned their posts." On Monday, July 5, the county court was in session, and a group of citizens went before the court to ask that funds for the expense of a guard be appropriated. The county judges declined the request, deciding instead to move the prisoner for safekeeping to a jail in a neighboring county until the regular term of circuit court.

Upon learning of the court's refusal, a mob formed and took Milligan from the small posse of guards who remained. Knowing the fate that awaited him, the prisoner asked to be baptized before he was hanged, and the request was granted. He was taken to a small stream in the south part of Albany and baptized by the Rev. Hiram Warner, a minister of the Christian Church.

The prisoner was met at the water by his father, William Milligan, and the exchange of sad farewells between father and son was "deeply affecting."

But apparently not deeply affecting enough to sway the vengeful mob. While the group was still at the water, a prominent citizen of Albany made a speech trying to prevail upon the crowd to raise sufficient funds to guard the prisoner until his trial instead of hanging him. About two hundred dollars was raised among the crowd, and a runner was dispatched to the county court to see whether they would appropriate the balance necessary to guard Milligan until his court date. When the answer came back "No," the mob started with the prisoner toward the elm tree where Kessler had been strung up.

A dry suit of clothes was procured to replace the wet garments Milligan had worn for his baptism, and the "prisoner dressed to meet his doom." He was then drawn up on the same limb that had served as Kessler's makeshift gallows ten days earlier.

According to the 1882 county history, the mob that lynched Kessler and the one that lynched Milligan were composed largely of the same men. They nearly all came from northern Gentry County and southern Worth County. Many of them had attended the vigilante meeting at Oxford shortly before Timmons was killed, and some were prominent citizens.

So, it's not surprising that, even though both lynchings were done in public view, little was ever done to make the vigilantes answer for their extralegal deeds. In 1868, ten years after the lynchings, James W. Curry, who'd been a Union lieutenant-colonel during the Civil War, was indicted for murder in Gentry Country for his part in the mob action. The case was transferred to Worth County on a change of venue, though, and either he was found not guilty or the charges were dropped.

4

The Public Strangling of a Criminal

Murder of the Newlands and Hanging of Charles Waller

On Thursday, May 16, 1872, citizens eager to be "edified by the public strangling of a criminal" began pouring into Marshfield, Missouri, according to a *Springfield Leader* reporter, in anticipation of the execution of convicted murderer Charles Waller, scheduled for the following day. Continuing his description of the scene, the newspaperman said,

> As early as Thursday morning the more impatient to witness the tragic spectacle began to make their way into the place. As the day wore away, hundreds upon hundreds more came in, whole families in wagons and squads of men and boys afoot and on horseback. The surrounding groves and thickets became suddenly populated until by nightfall the town was invested with a crowd whose camp-fires seemed like those of a besieging army.

About the first of May, 1867, twenty-eight-year-old William Newland (name sometimes given as Newlon); his wife, Mary; and their one-year-old son left their home in Washington County, Indiana, with the idea of settling in Missouri or one of the other Southwestern states. They stopped over for a few months in Illinois, where they made the acquaintance of the forty-two-year-old Waller; his thirty-four-year-old wife, Hannah; their eighteen-year-old son, Zachariah; and four younger children. Newland, whose father, Richard, was a well-to-do farmer in Washington County, had a good sum of money with him, with which he planned to buy land. He gave day laborer Waller some work, and when he decided to resume his family's journey to the Southwest, he invited Waller and his family to accompany them, promising Waller a job when they reached their destination. Newland even provided Waller with a team and a wagon with which to make the trip.

Sometime during the early fall of 1867, the two families reached Dade County, Missouri, where they visited Samuel A. Harshbarger, a relative by marriage of William Newland. They stayed for a while in a house that Harshbarger owned, but, after Newland was unable to find suitable land in the Dade County area, his party soon set off again, heading southeast toward Ozark County.

On or about November 1, they stopped in Webster County near Hazelwood several miles southeast of Marshfield along the Hartville road (approximating current-day Highway 38), and Newland and Zach Waller went into the woods to go hunting. Young Waller came back to his family's wagon alone and told his father, "Well, it's done," or words to that effect. When Waller asked for clarification, Zach told him that he had killed Newland. (At least one report said the father killed Newland, but, in either case, the "Well, it's done" statement suggests that both Wallers were in on the conspiracy.)

Charles Waller determined that, in order to cover up the crime, they had to get rid of Newland's wife and child. Later that evening, he or his son slit Mrs. Newland's throat, and, according to Waller's later confession, Zach took the child off into the woods and came back by himself, having presumably killed the little boy, Samuel Lincoln Newland.

A few days after Mary Newland was killed, a woman's remains were found along the Hartville Road near Cantrell Creek a few miles southeast of Hazelwood. The woman's throat had been cut. A coroner's inquest could not determine her identity, and she was buried. Because both the victim and perpetrator remained unidentified, law enforcement and the citizenry did not become particularly aroused at first.

Then, in the spring of 1868, a man's decapitated and bullet-ridden body was found in some woods near the Hazelwood road about eight miles from Marshfield. He was also buried without being identified.

Shortly afterward, relatives of the Newlands back in Indiana became concerned for the well-being of the family, since they had not heard from them, and Newland's father asked Harshbarger to investigate. Learning of the mysterious murders in Webster County, Harshbarger traveled from Dade County, had the victims' bodies exhumed, and identified them, at least partly by their clothing.

The fact that Mr. and Mrs. Newland were found several miles apart is a mini-mystery. It's not clear whether the woman was killed near the same spot as her husband and her body then hauled a few miles and dumped or she continued the journey with the Wallers, willingly or unwillingly, after her husband went missing and was killed farther down the road, where her body was found. The body of little Samuel Lincoln Newland was never found.

The discovery of Mr. Newland's body and the identification of the two victims caused much alarm, and the Wallers were immediately suspected of both murders. They became the object of an intense manhunt, funded mainly by William Newland's father and carried out primarily by Harshbarger. Richard Newland put up a $500 reward for the capture of the villains, and that amount was matched by Webster County.

The Wallers were tracked to Ozark County, where Zach Waller had gotten married, but the family had already taken off by the time authorities got there. Harshbarger then traced the Wallers to Arkansas, but he found upon his arrival that they had already left. The only additional information he could glean was that Zach had continued south to Texas, while the rest of the family had "gone north."

Returning home, Harshbarger engaged a Dade County lawman to travel to Texas to try to hunt down Zach Waller with the promise of the $1,000 reward that had been offered. When the deputy got back to Missouri, he reported that he had captured the fugitive but that he had been forced to shoot and kill Waller when he tried to escape. The man was allowed to collect the $1,000 reward, but many people doubted his story from the very beginning.

Meanwhile, Sam Harshbarger was hot on the trail of Zach's parents. He tracked them to Rock County, Wisconsin, and then to Beaver Creek in the same state. From there, he traced them to Faribault, Minnesota, where, on August 18, 1870, he finally caught up with them, still in possession of some of Newland's belongings. Harshbarger captured them and started with the family back to Missouri. When the party laid over in Chicago on the 19th, a *Chicago Tribune* newspaperman described Charles Waller as a forty-five-year-old man with a "decidedly dejected" appearance, "a right hand sawed off above the knuckles," and "a mouthful of tobacco."

Harshbarger delivered the fugitives to Marshfield, where they were lodged in the Webster County Jail. Charles Waller was indicted for first degree murder during the spring of 1871, and his wife, Hannah, was indicted as an accessory. Waller was tried at the March 1872 term of court, and on Friday, March 29, the jury brought in a verdict of guilty. The next day, Waller was brought back into court, and Judge R. W. Fyan pronounced a sentence of death by hanging. The execution date was set for May 17. Cursing the verdict and those who had testified against him, especially Sam Harshbarger, Waller said he had been convicted by a "pack of damned lies" but that he was ready to die. "Bring on your rope!" he exclaimed.

Hannah, meanwhile, pled guilty to manslaughter and was given a three-year sentence in the state penitentiary. She was received at the Jefferson City facility on April 1, 1872. From her cell on May 9, she wrote to Governor Gratz Brown proclaiming her husband's innocence and pleading for mercy in his case as well as her own. Three weeks earlier, she had given birth, while in prison, to a new baby, and she asked to be released so she could tend to the newborn and to her other children. She enclosed a letter, dictated by her illiterate husband and transcribed by his lawyer, that she had received just days earlier. In the letter, Waller talked of meeting her in heaven and told her to follow the Lord's path. Hannah concluded her own letter to the governor with a final plea: "May God Direct your Honor in whatever way that is wright (sic) and just."

Brown received at least four other letters pleading for leniency toward Waller. Among the letters was one signed by nine citizens of Trimble County, Kentucky, where Waller was originally from. The signees said that all of Waller's Kentucky connections were "respectable people." The Trimble County citizens added that most of them knew Waller and doubted that he would have done on his own what he was convicted of and that he must have been "led on." Another of the letter writers was Waller's court-appointed attorney, William Lowe. He did not claim, like Hannah, that Charles Waller was innocent of the crime. In fact, he specifically refuted the claim that Waller had been "led on" by others, he said his client had received a fair trial, and he admitted that the evidence against Waller was very strong. Instead, Lowe based his appeal wholly on his opposition to capital punishment. Governor Brown, however, was unmoved by any of the letters, saying that he did not feel he should countermand a lawful verdict.

Waller had been receiving spiritual counsel since his conviction, mainly from the Rev. McCord Roberts, a well-known Baptist minister in Southwest Missouri. However, he continued steadfastly denying having committed the crime for which he was to pay the ultimate price, until about the first of May, when he finally admitted the deed. Still, he seemed to assign most of the blame to his son and refused to offer many details.

On the morning of Waller's scheduled execution, Friday, May 17, 1872, morbidly curious spectators continued pouring into Marshfield, adding to the crowd that had already gathered the day before. The *Springfield Leader* reporter observed,

> Friday morning was ushered in with a cloudy sky and every prospect of a rainy day, but even this, though it deterred many doubtless whom a more propitious day would have brought out, had no effect seemingly upon others, who from sunup continued pouring in from every road and by-way until the town, square and every street leading therefrom became crowded even to their fullest capacity. So large a gathering had probably never assembled in Marshfield before, nor the quiet little town assumed so gala-day an appearance. Such is the strange attraction of the gallows to those whose necks are out of the noose.

By noon, an estimated 5,000 to 7,000 people of "all ages and both sexes" had assembled to witness the drama of seeing a man hang. "It is scarcely an exaggeration," said the Springfield newspaperman, "to say that the entire population of the town were upon the grounds." To these were added thousands who had come in "from the country around and even from other counties."

Charles Waller had been eating and sleeping well, but on the morning of his scheduled execution, he refused breakfast, saying that he felt nauseous, and he said he had slept hardly at all the previous night. He also reportedly wailed in agony. By early afternoon, however, when his hands were bound and he was led outside the jail on the way to his doom, he had regained his composure. He was seated in the front of a wagon, along with two law officers and the Rev. Roberts. Members of the press and three doctors rode in the back of the wagon, which also carried Waller's coffin. A special guard of 100 men encircled the wagon to keep the eager crowd at bay as Waller's final journey began. A caravan of other vehicles, horsemen, and pedestrians followed the wagon, as it made its way toward Bald Hill, one mile east of town, where a scaffold had been erected.

When the solemn procession arrived at the scene,

Sheriff Andrew Harrison and his deputy, Jordan Johnson, led the condemned man to the scaffold, and Waller walked up the stairs to meet his fate with a firm step. When the sheriff asked Waller if he had any last words to say, he answered in the negative. A cover was drawn over his face and the noose adjusted around his neck. The Rev. Roberts offered a brief, final prayer, and then he and the lawmen stepped away from the platform. The sheriff pulled the lever, the trap fell at precisely 1:20 p.m., and Waller was dropped into the ever-after in front of the gaping crowd of curious onlookers. The fall broke his neck, and his heart stopped beating within two minutes. Thirteen minutes later, his body was taken down and placed in the plain, pine coffin. Waller was buried in a grave that had already been prepared just a few feet away from the scaffold. With this task completed, the masses who had assembled for the gruesome spectacle began to break up.

On August 14, 1872, Governor Brown pardoned Hannah Waller, and she was discharged after serving just four and a half months of her three-year sentence. What happened to her after her release has not been traced.

Meanwhile, Zach Waller continued on the lam, but Harshbarger proved to be a stubborn detective. Operating on the supposition that Waller was, in fact, still alive, he continued to run down a number of leads. Finally, in early 1877, Jordan Johnson, who'd moved up from Webster County deputy to assume the sheriff's position, received a telegraph message from Waller's estranged wife that her husband could be found in Florida. Sheriff Johnson traveled there, captured the fugitive, and brought him back to Marshfield, where he was lodged in the county jail on February 1.

Waller was indicted in April on a first-degree murder charge, but when his trial came up in September, he struck a deal to spare his life. Prosecutors hoped Waller would reveal the fate of the Newland child. Some people still held out hope that the little boy might have been kidnapped by Hannah Waller rather than murdered by her son and husband

and might, therefore, still be alive. Trusting that, at the least, Waller would reveal the whereabouts of the child's body, prosecutors agreed to take the death penalty off the table in exchange for a second-degree murder plea. Waller accepted the deal on September 27 and received a sentence of 40 years in prison, but he still refused to talk about the little boy.

Zach Waller was received at the state penitentiary in Jefferson City on September 29, 1877. He was discharged on July 4, 1889, having been pardoned by Governor David R. Francis after having served less than twelve years of his forty-year sentence.

Not long after his release, Zach Waller remarried and had a child, but he either cast off his second wife, like he had his first, or else she died. At the time of the 1910 census, he was 63 years old and living in Stoddard County, Missouri, with his thirty-year-old third wife and their five children, as well as Waller's son by his second wife. What happened to the convicted killer after 1910 has not been determined.

5

The Depraved Condition of Society

Murder of James Clark and Hanging of John W. Patterson

     After John W. Patterson was arrested in December of 1868 for killing James G. Clark in Henry County, Missouri, he confessed to the crime. He escaped though, before he could come to trial, and he was not heard from again until he was recaptured in Illinois twelve years later. By the time he went to trial in 1881, he'd changed his tune after a dozen years on the lam, vehemently maintaining his innocence.
     But all the witnesses at the coroner's inquest in 1868 and all the members of the coroner's jury were still alive. And they had long memories.
     In November of 1868, James G. Clark, residing near Roscoe in St. Clair County, made a trip to Sedalia to buy lumber for a building project on his farm. While in Sedalia he met a young man named John W. Patterson, who had a wagon and team available, and Clark hired Patterson to haul the lumber for him. After he'd completed his purchases and engaged Patterson as his teamster, Clark withdrew a large sum of money from the First National Bank in Sedalia.
     The pair started southwest toward Roscoe with the lumber in late November and spent the night of November 30 on Tebo Creek in eastern Henry County. Clark, not feeling well, stayed inside at the nearby home of an accommodating farmer. The next day, December 1, the journey resumed, and Clark stretched out to rest on the load of lumber. Near Cole's Store (i.e. Coal), the twenty-four-year-old Patterson brained his employer with a blunt object as he lay prone on the lumber and then hacked him to death with a hatchet. He also took Clark's money, which amounted to at least $400, and

took a watch off the body.

After dumping the dead man in a stand of timber nearby, the villain continued southwest along the road until he reached the Grand River in southern Henry County. Patterson had been sent to Sedalia by his father, Hezekiah Patterson of Jasper County, to haul furniture; so the young man obviously had second thoughts about returning with a load of bloodstained lumber. Near Brownington, the murderer got rid of the lumber and tried to trade the watch he'd taken from his victim. He then started back toward Sedalia. He stopped at Cole's Store to mail a letter to his father and arrived back in Sedalia on December 4.

Meanwhile, Clark's body was discovered on December 3. A man had seen Patterson drive into the brush and throw something off his wagon on the 1st but thought little about it until a day or two later, when some school children reported finding a pair of boots lying on the roadside near the same location. The man then went to the spot where he'd seen Patterson drive into the brush, and he found Clark's dead and mutilated body. The neighborhood was aroused, and the victim was recognized by the man Clark had stayed with on the night of the 30th.

Also found hidden in the brush was a bloody grain sack with splinters in it, suggesting that it had been used to wipe blood off the load of wood. Marked in ink on the bloody sack was the name "Hezekiah Patterson." The tracks of the wagon leading to and away from the murdered man's body were peculiar in that they were considerably wider than those made by most wagons.

An inquest was called at once, and the postmaster at Cole's Store remembered that a letter addressed to Hezekiah Patterson, the same person whose name was inked on the bloody grain sack, had been mailed at his store earlier the same day or the day before. The letter, having not yet left the store, was turned over to investigators, who opened it and found that Hezekiah Patterson lived in Jasper County, that the letter was written by his son John W., and that the son said he was on his way to Sedalia. In addition, people living northeast of Cole's Store recalled seeing a young man and an older man pass along the road with a load of lumber a few days earlier, and they had seen the same young man come back by later in the week by himself. Based on these findings, a warrant for the arrest of John W. Patterson was issued by a local justice of the peace.

The roads were muddy from recent rains, and the peculiar, wide wagon tracks were easily picked up in the mushy ground. One party followed the tracks to Brownington and found the site where the bloodstained wood had been dumped, while another party trailed Patterson to Sedalia and turned the warrant for his arrest over to Pettis County sheriff William Paff. Patterson's wagon and team were located at a local livery, where he'd left the wagon to have the wheels cut down to normal size.

Patterson himself was traced to the Central Hotel, where Paff arrested him on the evening of December 4, still in possession of a pocketbook and most of the money he'd taken from Clark. At the time of his arrest, Patterson was described as "small in stature, and of rather effeminate appearance." He admitted the murder but claimed that he had an accomplice. No one believed the claim, because nobody had seen anyone else besides his victim in Patterson's company at any time.

The next day, December 5, Sheriff Paff and deputies took the prisoner back to the scene of the crime where he was indicted by the justice who'd issued the warrant. Patterson was then taken on to Clinton and turned him over to Henry County law officers. On the way, Patterson gave a fuller confession, claiming at first that he'd killed Clark in self-defense before admitting that he'd killed him for his money.

Patterson was placed in jail at Clinton to await the action of a grand jury. On January 19, 1869, from his Henry County Jail cell, he wrote a letter addressed to the young men of Jasper County and mailed it to a newspaper in Carthage, which published it shortly thereafter.

He began the letter by saying that he expected to have already paid with his life for his "disregard for human and divine laws" by the time the letter was published. Quoting several Bible verses, he admonished his young readers to shun the road he had traveled and, instead, to keep on "the path of moral rectitude." He said young people needed to guard against even minor transgressions like Sabbath breaking and disobedience to parents because the transition to evil was so gradual. He also exhorted them to sobriety, claiming that intoxicating liquors had excited his brain, dethroned his reason, and made him "become a murderer." He concluded by saying that he did not wish to cover up his crimes because he hoped that the downward spiral of his life might serve as a warning to others.

When Patterson's case came up at Clinton not long after he wrote his letter, he was granted a change of venue to Morgan County and was transferred to the county jail at Versailles. The calaboose where he was housed was a "rickety building," and he soon escaped, despite the fact that he was supposedly closely guarded. A reward was offered for his recapture, but he disappeared and was not seen again in Missouri for over ten years.

About six years after he escaped, his father died in Jasper County, and Amos Hoag, who shared Hezekiah Patterson's Quaker faith, was appointed administrator of the estate. Found among the papers of the deceased was a letter from John W. Patterson, who was living in Illinois at the time. E. S. Pike, a Carthage detective, learned of Patterson's general whereabouts through Hoag and, working in conjunction with the Henry County prosecuting attorney, set out to track the fugitive down. Patterson was finally located in the summer of 1880 in Livingston County, Illinois, where he'd been living under the name John W. Williams since shortly after his escape. He had a twenty-three-year-old wife and a newborn child.

Pike and a Livingston County deputy sheriff went to where Patterson, a well digger, was at work near Strawn,

Illinois, on the evening of August 20. Seeing that the man did not closely match the description of the fugitive he'd been given, Pike engaged the well digger in conversation, hoping to elicit some revealing information. Finally the detective asked the man whether he'd ever been to Carthage, Missouri.

After hesitating a moment, the wanted man replied, "What business is it of yours?"

"Are you not John W. Patterson?" Pike demanded.

The fugitive turned white upon hearing his real name, and the deputy immediately drew his revolver, placed him under arrest, and put him in handcuffs. As he did so, Patterson broke down and admitted his identity. He said he'd intended to go back and give himself up four years earlier.

Patterson was lodged in a local jail for the night and brought back to Missouri a day or two later. A new murder indictment was issued in Henry County, and Patterson's trial began there in April of 1881 with his wife and young child in attendance. Having retracted his earlier confessions, Patterson said he saw James G. Clark in Sedalia during the time in question, but he claimed that he declined Clark's offer to hire him as a teamster and did not leave town with him. All the witnesses who'd testified back in 1868 were present to once again give their testimony, and they told a much different story. The defendant was convicted on April 23 and sentenced to hang on June 10.

After the verdict, Patterson's wife took their baby boy and went back to Illinois. Although the couple wrote a few letters back and forth, they never saw each other again.

The defense filed a motion for a new trial, but it was overruled. Patterson's attorneys then appealed to the Missouri Supreme Court, which issued a stay until June 25. The high court later granted another stay until July 22 to allow more time for the justices to consider the case. When they finally ruled, they sustained the lower court's decision and ordered that the execution proceed as scheduled on July 22.

In June, Patterson wrote a detailed letter declaring his

innocence. He renewed his claim that he had a partner, and he said it was the partner who actually committed the crime. When he had confessed, Patterson said, he'd simply adopted the story that his accomplice had told him. The prisoner said he had not seen his accomplice since a day or two after the crime and that he did not even recall his name.

JOHN W. PATTERSON.

Patterson shortly before he was executed. *From the Sedalia Bazoo.*

Then, a week or two before his execution date, Patterson and his lawyers received intelligence that a man from the Granby, Missouri, vicinity had confessed on his death bed a few years earlier to killing a man named Clark "on the prairie" north of Granby several years prior to his dying statement. After investigating the matter, the Newton County prosecutor contacted Henry County authorities to inform them that the story might have some merit. Based on this glimmer of hope, one of Patterson's attorneys made a last-minute trip to Jefferson City seeking a stay of execution, but the governor denied the request.

In the days leading up to his scheduled execution, Patterson resisted offers of spiritual counseling. When he was moved to a different cell and put on a death watch on Wednesday, July 20, he finally agreed to see a minister. The Rev. J. M. Pierce visited him in his cell, but the prisoner steadfastly refused to confess his crime or to accept spiritual solace. That night, though, he tried to "beat out his brains" against the iron bars of his cell before guards intervened.

Patterson awoke at 5:00 a.m. on Friday, the 22nd. When several newspapermen visited him in his cell about an hour later, he said he resented a report one of them had written that he had "wilted down" and asked for a minister. The prisoner explained that he was asked repeatedly if he wanted a minister and that he finally told one of the petitioners they could send one if they wanted but that he didn't request one.

Asked how it could be that he had previously confessed to killing Clark but was now vehemently pro-claiming his innocence, Patterson explained that he only said what his interrogators wanted him to say to get them to leave him alone: "I was bothered to death with questions, and did not count the cost at the time." This time, instead of trying to blame his "accomplice" for the crime, Patterson latched on to the story out of Newton County that the man from Granby was Clark's real killer.

On the evening of the 21st, people had poured into Clinton, and they continued to do so throughout the morning of the 22nd, many coming by special trains from Sedalia and from Fort Scott, Kansas, until there were an estimated 5,000-

10,000 people gathered to witness the execution. Early Friday, they started assembling on the grounds where the scaffold had been erected a quarter of a mile west of Clinton.

An armed guard of about forty men escorted Patterson, as the procession to the scaffold began about 11:15 a.m. Crowds of people lined the streets all along the way, and then fell in behind the melancholy parade and followed the prisoner to his doom, eager to watch a man get choked to death. Editorializing against the morbid curiosity of the many people drawn to Clinton to see Patterson die, the hometown *Clinton Advocate* said, "It bespeaks to our mind a depraved and diseased condition of society that brings together such a crowd to witness his execution."

At the scaffold, Patterson mounted the steps with a firm stride, accompanied by the Rev. Pierce, Sheriff Ambrose Hopkins, and several other officials. After Pierce offered a prayer, the prisoner was asked if had anything to say. He thanked Hopkins, his attorneys, and the rest of his friends for the kindness they'd shown him and shook hands with those on the scaffold. The sheriff read the death warrant and then led Patterson to the trap, where he was bound, the black cap was placed over his head, and the noose adjusted around his neck. Raising a hatchet, Hopkins proclaimed, "John W. Patterson, may God have mercy on your soul." Then the hatchet fell, cutting the rope that held the trap in place, and Patterson, in the words of the *Sedalia Weekly Bazoo*, sank "with a sickening jerk into the misty beyond."

When the Rev. Pierce came down from the scaffold, someone asked him, according to the *Bazoo*, whether he thought Patterson was prepared to die, and the preacher answered, yes, "he thought Patterson would die happy but that, if he ever saw a man with a heart of stone, Patterson was the man."

Exhibiting the kind of ghoulish attention to detail that the *Clinton Advocate* editor would have no doubt found repulsive, the *Bazoo* newspaperman recorded the exact number of Patterson's heart beats per minute, as announced

by the attending physician, from the time the condemned
man dropped through the chute until he was pronounced dead
after thirteen minutes. The body was then taken down and
placed in a crude coffin. It was buried locally, since
Patterson's wife had not responded to inquiries about the
disposition of the body.

6

Taken Up

The Lapine Family Murders and the
Hanging of Armstrong and Jolly

When Washington County sheriff John Clark and his deputies trailed John Armstrong and Charles Jolly into neighboring Jefferson County in late November 1870, after the two villains had slaughtered five people, including Louisa and Mary Christopher, the lawmen stopped near Hematite at the home of the young women's mother to inform her of the tragedy. The officers were surprised, according to the *Washington County Journal*, by the mother's stoical manner and indifferent reply: "Well, I knew they were bad girls, but I think the two men have done enough now; they ought to be taken up."

And that's exactly what happened. Tried and convicted of first degree murder, Armstrong and Jolly were sentenced to hang and were "taken up" at Potosi in late January of 1871, just two months after their heinous crime.

On Saturday, November 19, 1870, forty-year-old Armstrong and thirty-five-year-old Jolly, lead miners living north of Potosi, had gone into town to sell their mineral. Also with them was Jolly's sixteen-year-old brother, Leon. The men spent the day drinking "bad whiskey" and then started back toward home, still imbibing from a jug of whiskey they'd purchased in Potosi.

About a mile and half north of Potosi, they stopped at the home of fifty-year-old David Lapine, who was their cousin, all of the men being French Creoles. Living with Lapine as his wife was twenty-three-year-old Louisa "Fanny" Christopher, and the couple had a small child together. Also living with the family was Fanny's twenty-two-year-old sister, Mary Christopher, and her baby.

Lapine had worked the mines in the area for many years and was considered an innocent old man, but the women of the house bore an indifferent reputation, at best. According to the *St. Louis Democrat*, the "miserable cabin of only one room," which they called home, "was frequently the resort of miners of the lowest class, who visited it for the basest purposes." Using understatement to effect, another report said the character of the female occupants of the cabin could not stand comparison with that of Diana or Caesar's wife. (Diana was the virgin goddess of childbirth and womankind in Roman mythology, and Caesar's wife was held to be above suspicion.)

Armstrong and Jolly, according to a New York newspaper, were themselves "notorious for their dangerous and worthless character." They had both been married but didn't live with their wives, and neither their wives nor any other family members took much interest in them. A local report confirmed that they were "of a low degree" and added that they had recently set fire to a house and stolen its contents, consisting of some lead ore and twenty-five or thirty dollars.

Arriving at the Lapine place, Armstrong and Jolly went inside, while Jolly's teenage brother stayed outside in the wagon. After a while, Leon Jolly got cold and stepped out of the wagon to go inside. Approaching the cabin, he was startled by loud, threatening curses coming from within. Afraid to open the door, he looked through a crack in the wall and was horrified by the scene he saw unfolding.

Armstrong and Charles Jolly were engaged in a heated argument with Mary Christopher. Lapine tried to intercede on his sister-in-law's behalf, and Jolly drew his revolver and shot him four times, killing him almost instantly. When Fanny Christopher rushed to her husband's aid, Jolly knocked her down and then shot and killed her, too. In the meantime, Armstrong picked up an ax and hit Mary in the head with it. He then chopped her head off and also severed the heads of the previous two victims. The two children, aroused from their beds by the commotion, made a dart for freedom but never reached the door. Armstrong struck one of them in the head with the ax, while Jolly picked the other one up and hurled it against the stone hearth, dashing its brains out.

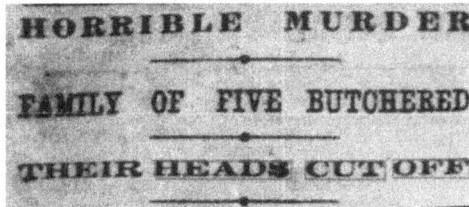

HORRIBLE MURDER

FAMILY OF FIVE BUTCHERED

THEIR HEADS CUT OFF

Headline from the *New Orleans Republican* announces Lapine murders.

The monstrous villains then set fire to the cabin and burned it to the ground with the bodies inside. Meanwhile, Leon Jolly slipped back to the wagon and pretended to be asleep when his brother and John Armstrong returned from their deadly work.

The murderers drove to the nearby home of Jolly's brother-in-law, arriving about midnight Saturday night. They stayed there until early Monday morning, and then, leaving Leon Jolly behind, they started north into Jefferson County on foot.

Because Lapine's cabin was in an isolated part of the country, the crime scene was not discovered until late Monday morning, November 21, about thirty-six hours after the murders. An alarm was raised, and the entire community flocked to the scene. Foul play being evident, authorities were notified, and Sheriff Clark, Dr. J. A. Bell, justice of the peace Michael Malony, and several Potosi citizens repaired to the scene, where, in the words of the *Washington County Journal*, they found evidence of "one of the most cruel and bloody tragedies known to the history of any civilized country."

The five bodies found among the ruins of the cabin

were virtually unrecognizable, but Dr. Bell, aided by the gathered neighbors, made tentative identifications upon close inspection. Sheriff Clark, with a few citizens serving as deputies, immediately started interviewing neighbors and interrogating possible suspects. One of those detained was Leon Jolly, and he readily confessed that he had witnessed the crime. A hastily convened coroner's jury concluded that the five victims had come to their deaths at the hands of John Armstrong and Charles Jolly.

After hearing Leon Jolly's story, the sheriff and two deputies set out on horseback on the trail of the murderers Monday evening, November 21. The search took them to several communities and residences in Jefferson County before the fugitives were finally located at what was known as the Italian Settlement about forty miles northeast of the crime scene. They were arrested late Tuesday afternoon at the home of Lucas Bellacamba, with whom Charles Jolly had recently lived. The captives were guarded overnight at the nearby home of a man who'd helped make the arrest. They were brought back to Potosi on Wednesday the 23rd and lodged in the Washington County Jail.

On the same day, the remains of the murdered family were brought to Potosi in a box and buried in a common grave at the town cemetery.

Armstrong and Jolly had a preliminary hearing the next day, November 24, before Justice Malony, and they were remanded to Sheriff Clark's care to await the action of a grand jury.

Late on the night of November 26, a mob gathered in front of the jail and demanded the prisoners be turned over to them, but Sheriff Clark, posted at a second-floor window of the adjacent courthouse, refused. Fearing just such vigilantism, he had posted a strong guard at the windows and doors of the courthouse, and, backed by his deputies, he ordered the crowd to disperse. When the would-be lynchers instead kept demanding the keys to the jail, Clark ordered his deputies to fire over the heads of the mob. In response to the warning shots, the vigilantes fired four or five shots at the lawmen. Clark then ordered his men to open fire on the crowd. The hail of bullets that rained down on the crowd killed one young man, wounded several other men, and sent the mob scattering in every direction. Chastened but outraged at the sheriff and his deputies, the vigilantes dispersed.

The next day, the sheriff gathered every able-bodied man he could to guard the prisoners. Later the same day, a militia detail of thirty soldiers furnished by the Missouri governor took Armstrong and Jolly to St. Louis for safekeeping.

They were brought back to Potosi under a similar escort around the middle of December. Leon Jolly was the primary witness against them at their trial, which began on December 21, and the next afternoon the jury convicted them of first-degree murder after deliberating only three minutes. When the verdict was announced, Armstrong and Jolly "showed no emotion," according to the *St. Louis Democrat*, "their faces wearing the same expression of stolid indifference habitual with them." Judge J. H. Vail sentenced the prisoners to die by hanging on January 27, 1871, and they were again taken to St. Louis to await their date with death.

On January 26, 1871, the day before they were scheduled to hang, a *New York Herald* reporter called at the St. Louis jail, a "miserable building...not commodious enough for village purposes," and visited "the semi-brutal, unintelligent convicts—the lowest specimens of intellectual humanity, though in physique fair specimens enough of the wild beast."

The newsman described Jolly, to whose cell he was led first, as "a tall, athletic young man" who was "roughly clad" with "a soft hat, slouched on his forehead, from under which a tangled lock of hair hung down to his eyebrows. His costume, his underclothing especially, was filthy in the extreme, showing that he had not drawn much upon the resources of the Mississippi since his incarceration." Saying they were going to die for something they didn't do, Jolly denied that he and Armstrong had committed the crime of which they had been convicted. He claimed his kid brother had been paid off to testify against them.

Escorted to the other murderer's cell after his visit with Jolly, the reporter described Armstrong thus:

> He was stouter and older man than Jolly, but infinitely more forbidding in appearance. He was square-shouldered, rather heavily built, and might be thirty-six years old, if one could discover any index of age or youth in the mass of squalor and brutishness which the man presented. He was, if possible, more dirty and forlorn-looking than his comrade. A broad, flat, battered nose...disfigured his face. He wore a tattered suit of Confederate gray. A short cloak, hanging loosely on him, of the same color, without a collar, was rolled up tight about his neck, and secured with numerous cords. He wore a tattered, greasy, broad-leafed military hat, drawn down over his right eye, which I soon discovered was totally blind. But the most disgusting feature about him was his nails, which were like those of a bird of prey.

Armstrong, like Jolly, denied the pair's guilt. He admitted they had been in Potosi on November 19, but he said they did not visit the Lapine cabin that night. He said Lapine was his cousin and that he had no quarrel with him or his family. He added that it could have been anybody who killed the family. "Everyone went to that place," he declared, "niggers and all. It was no better than a whorehouse."

The next morning at 8:00 a.m., Armstrong and Jolly were put aboard an Iron Mountain Railroad train bound for Potosi and death. The prisoners were handcuffed to each other, and their legs were chained. The guard detailed to escort them included Sheriff Clark and a posse of deputies. The train arrived in Potosi about noon on the 27th.

The condemned men were led from the railroad station to the courthouse grounds, where a gallows had been erected beside the jail. A crowd of about 3,000 people, coming from miles around, turned out to witness the public execution. "Several well dressed women...were in the crowd," noted the *Herald* reporter, who'd made the trip from St. Louis with the prisoners. The east coast newspaperman continued his description:

> Children of all ages were there, with their mothers; and there was as little pity in the hearts of the one as the other.... The people were jocose. They laughed and talked as folks would in a country theatre. The disposition to mob law vanished when they found that, for the first time in the history of the wild mining region, men were really to be hung according to law. Judge Lynch had always taken this business in hand.

One of Jolly's sisters wept bitterly when she visited him before he was taken to the gallows, but he showed little emotion. Father Michael O'Reilly, one of two priests who had accompanied the condemned men from St. Louis, convinced Jolly to speak to his kid brother, Leon, and they exchanged a few words but were "not looking very lovable" when they parted. Neither Jolly's father nor Armstrong's mother were in attendance, although they both lived nearby.

Sheriff Clark and his armed posse led the prisoners up the steps to the scaffold, twenty feet above the ground, at about 1:00 p.m. The final ceremonies were brief. Armstrong's and Jolly's legs were pinioned, and Father O'Reilly made a brief statement saying that the condemned men neither admitted nor denied their guilt. Clark then read the death warrant and asked the prisoners if they had any last words. They declined to speak but shook hands with the sheriff.

The black caps were then drawn over their faces, and Clark, using an ax, cut the rope that held the trap door in place. Jolly's neck was broken by the nine-foot fall, his head nearly torn from his body. He died instantly, but the noose around Armstrong's neck slipped, and he swung for a few minutes before life was extinct.

7

Dead! Dead! Dead!

Murder of James Hughes and Lynching of Jacob Fleming

After Jacob Fleming shot and killed James Hughes at Osceola, Missouri, in mid-June of 1871, Fleming was quickly arrested and lodged in the St. Clair County Jail. Editor T. C. Davis noted in the next edition of the *Osceola Herald* that there was serious talk in the immediate aftermath of the crime of lynching Fleming but that "wise counsel" had prevailed and dissuaded those "rash enough to engage in such an act" from carrying out their purpose. The editor felt sure that Fleming would now have a fair and impartial trial and that justice would be served in the case.

As it turned out, Editor Davis's faith in the "law-abiding citizens" of Osceola was premature.

On Saturday June 17, Hughes and Fleming had been among a group of men drinking in the middle of the afternoon at the Arcade, an Osceola saloon operated by John Anderson. Hughes was a Union veteran who had been seriously wounded at the Battle of Stone River and left crippled. He had a wife and two kids in Ohio, but he had been living in St. Clair County for some months in preparation of bringing his family to the area. He was described as a quiet, inoffensive man who normally didn't drink. On this occasion, though, he was somewhat inebriated but not obnoxiously so. The twenty-four-year-old Fleming, on the other hand, was considered a desperado and a bully.

Hughes and Fleming exchanged words, although the exact nature of the brief argument is uncertain. One report said that Fleming asked Hughes to play poker with him and that Hughes replied that he only played a straight game or only played "straight poker," implying that he thought

Fleming might play a crooked game. Fleming retorted that *"draw* poker" was his game and, as if to illustrate the remark, drew his revolver and started shooting.

Whatever the cause of the dispute, all accounts agree that, after a brief exchange of words between the two men, Fleming pulled out his pistol and shot the unarmed Hughes twice from close range, once through the jaw or lower part of the face and once through the throat. Hughes fell to the floor, gravely wounded. Downtown citizens, drawn by the sound of the gunshots, rushed to the scene and gathered with saloon patrons around the fallen man. When they first arrived, Hughes was apparently lifeless, but he soon revived. Climbing to his feet, he demanded that somebody give him a gun so that he might go after Fleming, who was still in the saloon talking to the bartender. Some of the men around Hughes tried to restrain him, but he broke away and made some "delirious demonstrations" before again sinking to the floor.

The gravely wounded man was moved at first to an open doorway of the saloon and then to a neighboring building, where he was laid out on a workbench and attended by a physician. Over the next couple of hours, he seemed to revive somewhat, and he was taken to the home of M. B. Stewart, where he had been staying. He died there about forty-five minutes later, or about three and a half hours after he'd been shot.

A coroner's inquest was held over Hughes's body almost immediately after he died. Six different men who had been in the saloon at the time of the shooting gave testimony. Most said they had not even realized there was an argument between Hughes and Fleming until they heard the first shot. Two or three of them said they then turned in time to see Fleming fire the second shot from point-blank range, after which Hughes fell to the floor.

Only one witness, Thomas Brown, was close enough to the action to give any testimony relevant to the nature of the quarrel that led to the shooting. He said that he and

Hughes were playing pool on a pigeon-hole table and started toward the bar together. Hughes said something to Brown, and Fleming, who was nearby, interjected, demanding to know whether Hughes had spoken to him. Gesturing toward Brown, Hughes replied, "No, I'm speaking to this man. It's his treat."

Although Hughes's suggestion that Brown would buy the next round was no doubt meant as a joke, Brown apparently took exception to it. He said to Fleming that Hughes seemed to know a lot about his (Brown's) business. Fleming agreed, and he and Hughes then started arguing. The next thing Brown knew, Fleming had his arm extended toward Hughes, and Brown heard two shots but claimed not to have actually seen a weapon.

Fleming, a husband and a father of two small children, was arrested on Saturday, shortly after the shooting, and placed in the St. Clair County Jail. Later that night, rumors that a mob might take the law into its own hands spread, but law enforcement officers appealed for calm and nothing happened. A grand jury indicted Fleming for first degree murder the following week, but when the case was called on June 28 during a special session of the St. Clair County Circuit Court, he was granted a change of venue to neighboring Benton County.

The *Osceola Herald* reported the change of venue the next day, June 29, 1871, saying that Fleming would soon be transferred to Benton County for an August trial. Incensed by the prospect that Fleming might get away with murder if his trial was moved to Warsaw, a St. Clair County "vigilance committee" decided to act. Their determination that Fleming should pay for his crime was no doubt steeled by his reputation for prior bad acts. He had joined the Union militia near the end of the Civil War and reportedly participated in several killings, house burnings, and similar acts. Then, shortly after the close of the war, he supposedly killed a man at Osceola and was not even arrested for the crime. To top things off, just five or six months before the Hughes affair,

Fleming was said to have fired shots at a man in Roscoe, a small community in St. Clair County, shooting off part of the man's ear.

In the wee hours of Friday morning, June 30, two groups of disguised men, totaling about 100, rode into Osceola from opposite directions and converged on the jail. The vigilantes seemed to be well organized. Surrounding the building, they threw out pickets and allowed no one to approach, while others among them were assigned different tasks, such as holding the horses.

Sheriff Samuel Donovan promptly appeared on the scene and asked that two prominent citizens of Osceola be allowed to address the vigilantes. Someone in the mob replied that "they were not there for the purpose of listening to speeches," and "their language was too plain to be misunderstood," according to Editor Davis. One of the vigilantes stepped forward and demanded of Sheriff Donovan that he hand over the keys to the jail, but the sheriff refused. The mob then forced open the jail door with several blows from a sledge hammer. Locating Fleming's cell, they knocked off the lock with several more "well-directed blows of the sledge" and "in less time than it takes to tell it, emerged from the jail with Fleming in their midst and a rope already about his neck."

SUMMARY EXECUTION OF JACOB FLEMING.

He is Taken from Jail and Hung by a Body of Disguised Men.

Fleming's lynching made headlines in the local *Osceola Herald.*

The prisoner reportedly made no appeal and met his fate stoically. The mob marched him to a brick yard about 300 yards from the jail and strung him up to a cross beam that had originally formed part of the brick shed. "Jacob

Fleming was soon dangling a lifeless corpse," Editor Davis concluded.

One of the vigilantes pronounced Fleming "Dead, dead, dead!" and the mob then began to disperse. After they left, the acting county coroner cut Fleming's body down and took it to the courthouse, where an inquest was held shortly after daylight. No one was able (or willing) to identify any of the participants in the mob action, and the coroner's jury concluded that Fleming had come to his death at the hands of parties unknown. Nobody at the inquest blamed Sheriff Donovan for allowing the vigilantes to take the law into their own hands because he had been "forced to yield to circumstances which he could not successfully resist." Fleming's body was buried later the same day, June 30.

In reporting Fleming's lynching in early July, Editor Davis condemned the general idea of mob violence, but he admitted that in this particular case "the point had well nigh been reached beyond which forbearance would have ceased to be a virtue." Fleming was a notorious desperado, Davis explained, and the killing of Hughes was a "deliberate, heartless, unprovoked and cowardly murder." In addition, Davis pointed out that "a long list of unpunished crimes" had been committed in St. Clair County in recent years, and it was, therefore, understandable that the vigilantes had concluded that "assassins should no longer go unwhipt of justice."

Davis's opinion was shared by a large portion of the St. Clair County citizenry. On July 11, a mass meeting was held at the courthouse in Osceola, and those in attendance adopted a series of resolutions pertaining to the recent vigilante action. One resolution fully endorsed the hanging as "just and necessary to the peace of this community, and as a warning to all murderers in the future."

8

A Busy Week

The Spencer Murders and Lynching of Bill Young

William "Bill" Young must have set some sort of record for momentous events happening to the same person in a short period of time. In the space of five days in late October of 1879, he was acquitted of multiple murder, got married, went to Iowa on a honeymoon, and came home to Missouri to be lynched.

When the mob was getting ready to hang him near Luray in Clark County, he declared that he was perfectly innocent of the crime he'd been accused of committing. The mob wouldn't listen, though, because they knew Bill Young. He was the same man who'd been tried and convicted of another murder in the Luray vicinity almost twenty years earlier, received a measly eight-year prison sentence, and got out after three. And now he was about to get off scot free after slaughtering a family of five. The mob meant to see to it that he didn't.

As it turned out, though, the ringleader of the mob might have been as big a scoundrel as Bill Young.

Young first got into serious trouble with the law in October of 1860 when he was a young married man of twenty-two living along the Fox River near Chambersburg in northern Clark County. Among his neighbors were John Baird and the Malloy brothers. John and Edward Malloy leased their farm from James Whiteford, who lived in Canada but made periodic trips to the area to check on his property. When Whiteford visited Missouri in the fall of 1860, the thirty-year-old Baird organized a posse of his neighbors, including Bill Young, to arrest the Canadian, because he claimed the fifty-two-year-old Whiteford had stolen a mare from him on a previous visit.

Despite the fact that some people thought Baird had sold the mare and despite the fact that he lacked a warrant, he succeeded in rounding up four other young men besides Young; William White, Solomon Fouts, James Reeves, and Isaac Stephenson; to help him make the "arrest." The posse called at the Malloy residence on Saturday evening, October 6, and took Whiteford into custody, but instead of taking him to a justice of the peace, they took him out and tied him to a tree. Bill Young compelled Reeves at gunpoint to lash Whiteford with switches in a futile effort to get him to confess to horse theft. Young also stole $150 from Whiteford's pocket while he was tied up.

The gang finally untied Whiteford and took him to Baird's house, where they held him prisoner. Baird and Young swore the other four "deputies" to silence at the point of a gun, and Reeves and Stephenson left the next morning. The remaining four men, realizing the trouble they could be in for what they'd done in their vain efforts to obtain a confession, decided to put the main witness against them out of the way. They took Whiteford out on Sunday night, put a rope around his neck, threw it over a tree limb, and pulled him up. When they let him down, he was still alive; so they pulled him up again. The second time they let him down, he was unconscious, but his heart was still barely beating. John Baird then jumped up and down on top of his chest until life was extinct. The villains buried Whiteford nearby and gave out the story that he had escaped.

Stephenson, though, went to authorities a week later and told what he knew, and Reeves also turned state's evidence. Whiteman's body was discovered, and Baird, Young, Fouts, and White were charged with murder, with Baird as principal and the other three as accomplices. After a change of venue, Baird was convicted of first degree murder and hanged in Lewis County in April of 1861. Fouts was convicted of second-degree murder, and White was convicted of manslaughter. They received ten years and five years respectively in the state penitentiary.

Bill Young was tried in neighboring Knox County on a change of venue in June of 1861, convicted of second-degree murder, and sentenced to eight years in prison. He was pardoned by Missouri governor W. P. Hall and released on February 27, 1864, after serving less than three years.

Young returned to Clark County and took up residence in the Luray vicinity with his wife, Mary, and their son, John, who had been born shortly before Young went to prison. Several more children followed over the next decade, and Young became a prosperous farmer, although many people still considered him a dangerous man.

In January of 1877, Mary died, and from all appearances, her husband was grief-stricken by her death. However, the following month, a young, good-looking divorcee named Laura Sprouse moved in with Bill Young as his housekeeper, and some of his neighbors looked askance on the arrangement, especially coming so soon after Mary Young's death.

Whether Bill Young's housekeeper was also his paramour is not known for sure, but one thing is certain: Laura Sprouse would play an important role in Young's life over the next couple of years.

On the morning of August 3, 1877, the Lewis Spencer family was found slain at their residence about six miles north of Luray. Twenty-six-year-old Willis James, younger brother of Spencer's deceased wife, made the discovery when he arrived to help his brother-in-law harvest. James found his eighteen-year-old niece, Jane, and her little brother, Charles, in a bed downstairs with their heads bashed in. He found their sister, twenty-year-old Alice, in an upstairs attic with her skull crushed as well. Going to the barn, where forty-five-year-old Lewis Spencer and his older son, ten-year-old Willis, were accustomed to sleep during summer, James discovered the pair similarly treated. The two girls and the older boy were already dead, while the father and the younger son clung to life, but they, too, died by the time help could be summoned. An ax found at the house with pieces of hair matted in blood was thought to be the primary murder weapon, although a pitchfork was also wielded against the older boy. Spencer was known to keep large sums of money, and robbery was thought to be the motive for the killings.

No suspects were named at first, although there was a "strong suspicion," said one Clark County correspondent, that the murderers "belong to this county." Suspicion soon settled on Willis James, the kinsman who had discovered the bodies, and Elijah Spencer, Lewis Spencer's brother. There was insufficient evidence against Elijah Spencer to make an arrest, but James was taken into custody in early October of 1877 based on certain circumstantial evidence. When he came to trial in April of 1878, however, the case against him was dropped when a key piece of blood evidence could not be corroborated.

In October of 1878, over a year after the Spencer murders, a man named Daniel C. Slater arrived in Clark County, fresh from the Illinois State Penitentiary at Joliet by way of Mexico, Missouri. Adopting the name Frank Lane, the twenty-seven-year-old Slater claimed to be a detective, and he offered his services to the local anti-horse thief association to help track down the murderers of the Spencers. The organization refused to employ him, but some of the individual members subsequently hired him for the job. Lane, the "pseudo-detective," as a Mexico newspaper called him, first revived interest in Willis James and Elijah Spencer as possible suspects. When no new evidence came to light, he set his sights on Bill Young.

Young had started corresponding with a woman named Lydia Bray, who lived in his native Ohio, and during the holiday season of 1878-1879, he traveled back to Ohio for a visit. While he was gone, Lane and a young man named Walter Brown paid Laura Sprouse a visit at the Young residence and succeeded in eliciting incriminating testimony from her against Bill Young in the Spencer murder case.

The fact that Brown was a former beau of Laura's no doubt played a role in her willingness to talk about her employer. In fact, Laura later married Brown. Some observers at the time also speculated that Laura carried a torch for Young and felt betrayed by his interest in the Ohio woman. At any rate, Lane and Brown took Laura away from the Young farm in early January of 1879 and deposited her in a secret hiding place. About a month later, she appeared before a justice of the peace to swear out an affidavit charging Young with murdering the Spencer family. A warrant for Young's arrest was placed in the hands of Frank Lane, and he and his posse took the suspect into custody in late February. Young was lodged in the Clark County Jail at Kahoka to await arraignment.

In the lead-up to the hearing, rumors circulated that Laura Sprouse "knew all about the Spencer murder" and that the state had evidence that would "unavoidably fasten the guilt" on Young. A purported confession by a man recently sent to the state penitentiary from Clark County also implicated Young in the crime, but "the whole story is rather mixed up," said one report at the time.

After his initial examination in early March, Young was bound over to await the action of a grand jury. In April, the jury indicted him for murder. The trial was set for August but was continued until October at the defendant's request.

As the time for the trial approached, rumors of mob action circulated, and the prisoner was removed to the Macon County Jail for safekeeping. He was brought back to Kahoka in early October, and the trial got underway in the Clark County Circuit Court on the 6th.

Laura Sprouse was the state's star witness. She testified that she overheard Young plotting with other men to kill Spencer, that she accompanied him to the Spencer neighborhood a few days before the murders and he pointed out the Spencer residence as a "good place to get money," that he told her he was going to Spencer's when he left on the night of the murders, that he came home the next morning with blood on his overalls and shirt, that he later admitted the murders to her, and that he offered her $1,000 to provide him an alibi. She also said that Young tried to burn the bloody overalls but that she rescued them and later turned them over to Frank Lane as evidence.

Lane disappeared during Laura's testimony and was found several days later lying unconscious in the road a couple of miles outside Kahoka. When he revived enough to testify, he said he'd been attacked by three ruffians who'd taken the overalls from him, and the state suggested that the assailants were friends of Young.

The defense, on the other hand, claimed Young's prosecution was a frame-up instigated by Lane, a so-called detective who was more interested in collecting the reward money than in seeing justice done and who settled on Young as the prime suspect mainly because of his prior murder conviction rather than because of actual evidence in the Spencer case. Young's lawyers tried to impugn Laura Sprouse's testimony by arguing that she had been bribed and carefully coached by Lane. They also produced witnesses who disputed parts of the young woman's story, while the prosecution countered with its own witnesses to confirm parts of her story.

Attacking the detective's sleazy character, Young's attorneys called witnesses to show that twenty-eight-year-old D. C. Slater, alias Frank Lane, had recently been incarcerated at the Illinois State Penitentiary under yet another alias. The defense argued that the supposed assault on Lane was just a put-up job to give Lane an excuse for not being able to produce the incriminating overalls. Young's lawyers also attacked the dubious character of some of the state's other witnesses.

Arguments concluded in the Spencer murder case the evening of October 24, and the jury, after deliberating about an hour and a half, came back on the morning of the 25th with a not guilty verdict. Public reaction to the verdict was about equally divided among those who felt either that

Young was innocent or that there was at least a reasonable doubt of his guilt and those who felt sure he had killed the Spencers. Among the most adamant in the latter group was Frank Lane, who immediately began agitating for vigilante justice.

Meanwhile, Young celebrated his acquittal by getting married the next day, Sunday, October 26, in Clark County to his Ohio fiancée, Lydia Bray, who'd traveled to Missouri for the trial. The couple prepared for a short honeymoon to Keokuk, Iowa, about twenty-five miles away, and as they were leaving, Young was warned to stay away because of the excitement that was building against him. One of his attorneys, J. C. Coffman, also contacted him while he was in Keokuk and again warned him that it was not safe for him to return to Clark County.

Disregarding the warnings, Young said his home was at Luray and that was where he meant to live. He and his bride came back home on Wednesday, October 29, arriving about mid-morning. Shortly thereafter a messenger came out to the Young place about mile outside Luray to warn that the expected mob was forming, but Young stubbornly refused to take flight, announcing that he'd rather die defending his home and family than run. At the house with him and his wife were his four kids by his first marriage, a Mrs. Rowe and her three children, and Coffman.

The mob, led by Frank Lane and William "Buffalo Bill" Smith, approached and surrounded the home about 11:00 a.m. With Young and his oldest son, John, defending the house, the two sides had a standoff until afternoon, exchanging only a few random shots. Coffman then came out under a truce and was locked in a granary, as Young parleyed with the would-be lynchers. The mob, which numbered as many as 200 or more, invited the women and children to come out under a guarantee of protection, but only Mrs. Rowe and her children accepted the offer. Young agreed to pay all costs of his recent trial and to leave the territory if he and his family would not be molested, but he refused the mob's demand that he admit to the Spencer murders.

After the ceasefire ended, the vigilantes made a half-hearted effort to burn the occupants out of the house, but they soon extinguished the fire. Shortly thereafter, Young appeared at an upstairs window and was shot by one of Lane's henchmen. Not knowing how badly Young was injured, the mob waited a while before charging the house and forcing an entry. Lane and his men found Young lying on the floor upstairs with his wife and kids standing over him crying.

Young called for a picture of his first wife and kissed it affectionately. Lane shook hands with Young and allowed him to dictate a short biography of his life to two of the other vigilantes, who wrote the story down.

Locking Young's wife and kids in an upstairs room, the mob then took their prisoner downstairs and out into the yard. The vigilantes lined up, and Lane selected nine of them to carry out the lynching. Young's feet and hands were tied, and he prayed "in a very supplicating manner" as he was carried to a nearby orchard gateway and placed in a wagon. Allowed time to make a statement, Young launched into a rambling speech offering to help ferret out the Spencer murderers, but the angry mob told him that wasn't what they wanted to hear. They wanted to know who helped him kill the Spencers. "I am as innocent of that crime as the Angels in Heaven," Young answered.

Whether he was innocent or not, a halter was promptly tied around Young's neck, with Lane himself acting as "master of ceremonies," and the wagon was driven beneath the heavy gate. The other end of the halter was tied to the gate's crossbeam, and the wagon was driven out from under its human cargo at about 4:00 o'clock in the afternoon. The body swayed in the wind for about twenty minutes until the mob was convinced that life was extinct, and then they mounted their horses. Mrs. Young, who'd been released, came out of the house crying and beseeching the men to cut her husband's body down, but they galloped away instead.

BILL YOUNG'S FATE.

Tried for Murder, Acquitted on Saturday, Married on Sunday and Hanged on Wednesday.

Headline from the *La Plata (MO) Home Press* tells Bill Young's story

After the lynching, opinion was divided concerning the mob action, just as it had been concerning the outcome of the trial. Some people wholly approved of the hanging, and others, while not endorsing the summary method of disposing of Young, were glad to be rid of a man whom they considered a dangerous character. Still others, many of them friends of Young, considered the deed "a dastardly outrage."

A coroner's inquest was held the day after Young was killed, and the jury reached the innocuous conclusion that he had come to his death by hanging "at the hands of a mob," despite the fact Frank Lane and several other men had been cited by name in the evidence given to the jury.

If the coroner's jury would not act, Lydia Young decided to act on her own. She swore charges against Frank Lane and eight other men in the death of her husband, and they were arrested. When their preliminary examination came up on November 5, though, no one appeared to prosecute the case, and it was dismissed.

Exasperated by the failure of local authorities to bring Young's lynchers to justice, Missouri governor John S. Phelps sent his adjutant general to Clark County to insist on enforcement of the law, but, by now, Lane and his cohorts had been turned loose and could not be located.

Phelps responded on November 21 by offering a reward of $250 each for the arrest of Frank Lane and Buffalo Bill Smith. The two were arrested five days later and brought to Kahoka on the 27th. Taken before a justice, they waived examination and were released on bail of $7,000 each.

Their case came before a grand jury in April of 1880. Despite an admonition from Judge John C. Anderson that the circumstances surrounding Bill Young's lynching constituted premeditated murder, the jury failed to indict. Frustrated by the jury's refusal to act, Anderson transferred Lane and Smith's case to neighboring Scotland County, and the pair were indicted there in the late spring.

Lane and his sidekick were again nowhere to be found. Earlier in the year, while authorities were still trying to make the murder charge against Lane stick, the accused had been adding to his notoriety. He was suspected of being at the head of a bold robbery in Clark County, and soon afterward he absconded to nearby Illinois with a seventeen-year-old Clark County girl.

When Lane learned that the sheriff of Scotland County was hot on his trail, he deserted the girl and headed to Yankton, South Dakota. Going by the name Frank Hale, he was arrested there for forgery and lodged in the local jail. Armed with a description of the Missouri fugitive, the Yankton police suspected the bird they had caged was none other than Frank Lane, and they contacted the Scotland County sheriff, who traveled to South Dakota in early June to confirm the prisoner's identity and bring him back to Missouri. The girl Lane had jilted met the train carrying her erstwhile "husband" when it stopped at the depot in Memphis, Missouri. With pistol in hand, the angry young woman tried to board the train but was denied entrance, and it continued on to Mexico, where Lane was lodged in the Audrain County Jail for safekeeping.

Lane's lawyers filed a writ of habeas corpus seeking their client's release on the grounds that he could not be indicted in a county other than the one where the alleged crime was committed. The motion was denied, but on appeal, the Missouri Supreme Court ruled in November in Lane's favor. He was thus turned loose and never heard from again. And nobody ever paid for the lynching of Bill Young.

9

A Demoniac Case

Schuendler Murders and the Hanging of Thaddeus Baber

Thaddeus Baber was smitten with Elizabeth "Lizzie" Schuendler from the time he first met her in St. Louis about 1873. She was only fifteen or sixteen, but she had "already begun the downward course of life," according to the *St. Louis Post-Dispatch*. She'd worked as a call girl in the "assignation house" run by her mother, Fredericka Schuendler, and she had a baby boy by another man. But none of that mattered to the twenty-four-year-old Baber. As he later confessed, he knew Lizzie was "not the chastest woman in the world," but he still loved her.

Baber talked Lizzie into taking up with him, and, they lived together as man and wife off and on for the next several years. Thaddeus, or Dave as he was often called, worked as an apprentice plumber, and the couple lived for a year or two near the fair grounds on the outskirts of town. Baber wanted to marry Lizzie, and he treated her little boy as his own son. But Fredericka, who'd taken a dislike to Baber, opposed the match, and Dave and Lizzie often argued over what he saw as the interference of the "old woman."

In March of 1879, Baber started his own plumbing shop downtown at the corner of Sixth and Poplar, and he and Lizzie set up housekeeping in some adjacent rooms. Fredericka's place was just a few blocks away at 821 Fourth Street, and Lizzie would often drop by to see her mother. Sometimes she spent the night, and Fredericka continually encouraged her daughter to come back home permanently and work for her. Baber strongly opposed Lizzie's visits to her mother's "den of sin," and he grew increasingly bitter toward the old lady.

On Sunday, August 10, 1879, Lizzie and Dave had a violent quarrel, and she left to go stay with her mother, taking some of the couple's household goods with her. "Half crazed by the desertion," according to the *Post-Dispatch*, Baber "lay drunk Monday and Tuesday," trying to drown his misery.

Baber tried to get Lizzie to come back to him, but she either refused his request or wouldn't even see him. Despairing that Lizzie would ever return, he sold the remainder of his furniture on Wednesday, August 13, and bought a pistol.

On Thursday morning the 14th, though, he saw Lizzie in the French Quarter neighborhood and again tried to talk her into coming back home with him. She declined but "did not seem entirely averse" to the idea, according to Baber's later story, and agreed to meet him that evening at dusk outside her mother's place. He told her he'd bring her a new dress.

Baber showed up at the Fourth Street address on schedule and stood on the street in the rain waiting for Lizzie to appear. When she came to a window in a second-story room, he waved a handkerchief as a signal, but she retreated from the window without acknowledging him. Waiting despondently for Lizzie to come down or to reappear at the window, Baber grew convinced that she was with another man, and he became more and more jealous.

Shortly before 8:oo p.m., he went upstairs in a rage with his pistol in hand to see what was going on. At the top of the stairs he found Lizzie's mother seated in the parlor reading, and he asked to see Lizzie. What the old woman replied is not known, but whatever she said prompted Baber to level his pistol and shoot her in the head, killing her instantly. He then heard footsteps approaching from an adjoining room, whirled, and fired again just as the door swung open. The bullet struck Lizzie in the breast, and she collapsed to the floor gravely wounded.

Sketch of Thaddeus Baber from the *St. Louis Post-Dispatch*

Baber was arrested almost immediately by two officers who heard the shots and rushed to the scene. He freely confessed his guilt and "rather glorie(d) over the killing of the old woman," but he expressed deep regret about Lizzie. Claiming that shooting her was an accident, he said he thought she was with another man and that the footsteps he heard approaching were those of her gentleman caller. Baber also said, at first, that the old woman had "ripped out an oath" and reached for a revolver when he asked to see Lizzie, but he later dropped the claim of self-defense.

In reporting the crime the next day, the *Post-Dispatch* said Baber had made a name for himself "by blowing out the brains" of the notorious Madame Schuendler. "The case is a demoniac one throughout, and has seldom, if ever, been surpassed in the annals of crime."

Lizzie was rushed to the St. Louis City Hospital, where she lingered until Saturday morning, August 16. The body was then removed to the morgue, where a coroner's inquest was held the same day. Baber, who'd been wildly demanding to see Lizzie ever since the shooting, was finally allowed to view her body at the inquest. Brought into the room shackled, he "gave way at once," according to a special report to the *Chicago Tribune,* caught hold of one corner of the coffin, and "began to kiss the cold mouth of his mistress." Later, he "sank on his knees by the coffin and broke into convulsive sobs."

Baber remained at the inquest throughout most of the testimony. Lizzie's seven-year-old son sat next to the prisoner, and, upon growing tired, the lad curled up in his chair, put his head on Baber's arm, and went to sleep.

At Baber's preliminary hearing on August 21, the defendant waived examination and was committed to Murderers' Row in the St. Louis City Jail to await the action of a grand jury in October. His attorney indicated that he planned to pursue an insanity defense, suggesting that he had the "prettiest case" of lunacy on record.

The grand jury indicted Baber for first-degree murder in the case of Fredericka Schuendler, and his trial was set for June 1880. When the defendant appeared in court on June 14, he was described as "a stumpy little fellow with horny hands, a low forehead, wide temples, teeth like Dickens' Carker, shining black hair, close-cropped, and a moustache of the same color. His bandy legs are not commensurate with his tremendous chest, nor the length of his arms with his height." Baber was said to be of a sulky disposition upon first acquaintance but less so as one got to know him.

Baber's trial was continued until the November term, and when it resumed on the 20th of that month, Baber's lawyers presented their insanity case. Various witnesses, including the defendant's aged mother, Julia F. Baber, testified that Baber had suffered a severe blow to his head when he was a child and had to have a hole cut in his skull to relieve the pressure on his brain caused by the swelling. A silver plate had been placed in his skull to cover up the place where the trephining was done, but his lawyers argued that the operation had not been properly performed and that Baber's skull still pressed against his brain, causing him to have "spells."

Unswayed by the insanity defense, the jury came back on November 24, 1880, with a verdict of guilty as charged. Baber, who had remained calm throughout the legal proceedings against him, greeted the jury's announcement, according to the *Post-Dispatch*, "much the same as a person receiving an adverse decision in a wager."

About the time the trial concluded, a man came to the office of Baber's lawyer claiming to be Lizzie Schuendler's brother. He said that their parents had died when they were both infants, that they were taken in by relatives, but that Lizzie was shortly thereafter adopted by Mrs. Schuendler. He said he did not even know he had a sister until he was almost an adult and that he only recently learned of her whereabouts. An elderly St. Louis woman who had known Fredericka and her parents in Illinois, however, swore out an affidavit that Lizzie was, in fact, Fredericka's natural child. The man's claim was thus dismissed as a bogus attempt to lay his hands on part of the $2000 in cash and $5000 in personal property belonging to Fredericka that the public administrator had taken charge of after her death.

Baber's lawyers filed a motion for a new trial, which was overruled, but the verdict was then appealed. The Missouri Court of Appeals affirmed the verdict in October 1881, as did the Missouri Supreme Court shortly thereafter, and Baber's execution date was set for January 13, 1882. The defense's last-minute appeals to the Missouri governor for clemency or a postponement so that Baber's insanity plea could be thoroughly examined were likewise rejected.

On January 11, 1882, two days before Baber's date with death, Julia Baber visited her son in the city jail at the Four Courts Building, located at 12th and Clark streets. A *Post-Dispatch* reporter, who was present at the time, said the interview between mother and son was "a sad one," with Mrs. Baber folding her son in her arms and tears pouring down her cheeks.

Baber told the reporter he was not afraid of death and would sooner die than spend the rest of his life in prison.

Mrs. Baber again visited her son on Thursday, January 12, accompanied this time by the condemned man's sister. "The distressing scene of yesterday was re-enacted," said the *Post-Dispatch*.

Another man in the St. Louis jail, William Ward, was also scheduled to hang on the same day as Baber. On Thursday night, Baber was allowed into Ward's cell, where three ministers counseled and prayed with them until 10 p.m. After the spiritual advisors left, Baber read the Bible aloud to his illiterate cellmate, and the two men sang hymns together until the guards appeared to escort Baber back to his cell.

The next morning both men awoke early after a brief sleep. Baber smoked a cigar and joked to one of his guards that he was a plumber by trade but was "going to quit the business today." The two men again read the Bible and sang before taking breakfast. After the meal, they sang and read some more, Baber visited a couple of other cellmates to bid them goodbye, and the two condemned prisoners were again visited by a spiritual advisor.

Shortly after 8:00 a.m., the death warrants were read to Baber and Ward, their hands were tied, and they were placed at the head of a procession and marched to the gallows in the courtyard. The few hundred people who'd been allowed inside the enclosure surrounding the scaffold pressed in around the condemned men as they were led to their doom. When they reached the platform, a minister offered a prayer, and both Ward and Baber declined to make a final statement. The men's legs were pinioned and hoods placed over their heads, and the trap was sprung just after 8:30 a.m. They were pronounced dead after about ten minutes and their bodies cut down after fifteen.

In addition to the spectators who'd been given tickets to witness the execution of Baber and Ward, a large crowd milled around outside the jail, although not as large as the one that had assembled for a recent hanging at the same location. "The public is evidently becoming tired of hanging matinees as a public entertainment," said the *Post-Dispatch*.

After his hanging, Thaddeus Baber was buried in the Bellefontaine Cemetery in St. Louis later the same day.

What I Have Done Deserves Death

The Murder of the McLaughlin Girls and the Hanging of Oliver Bateman

On Sunday, August 31, 1884, John McLaughlin, who lived a quarter-mile northwest of Flag Springs in Andrew County, Missouri, left home with his wife and three of their children to visit the family of neighbor George Elrod, while two other children, daughters nine-year-old Austie and seven-year-old Adella, were allowed to walk to the Thomas Bateman home about a mile and a quarter west of the McLaughlin residence and spend part of the day there. (Contrary to newspaper reports at the time, there were more than five children in the McLaughlin family, and Austie and Adella were not the oldest.) When McLaughlin and his wife returned home late that afternoon and the girls weren't back yet, they grew anxious, and their concern heightened with each passing minute.

McLaughlin undertook an investigation and learned the girls had left the Bateman residence to go home about 2:30 in the afternoon. Members of the Eli Knappenberger family had seen them pass their house about 3:00 p.m. on their way home, but for some reason the girls never made it. Neighbors flocked to join the search for little Austie and Adella, scouring the woods and the fields, but to no avail. The hunt was finally called off after midnight, but it was resumed early the next day.

About nine o'clock Monday morning, September 1, the girls' bodies were found in a cornfield on the property of Dr. William A. Lockett, who lived about a quarter mile east of the Knappenberger place. Austie was found first, lying on her back with her arms and legs extended, and a bullet hole in her left temple. She had been "outraged" and her body mangled and carved with a knife. Her intestines bulged from three long gashes that ran from her breastbone to her waist, and her mouth was badly bruised. Adella was found about 100 yards from her older sister, nearer the road, suggesting she'd made a frantic run to try to escape. Her throat was cut from ear to ear, and she also had a slash on her right side.

Shortly after the bodies were found, they were removed to Flag Springs, and a jury under the direction of Andrew County prosecuting attorney and acting coroner Charlie Booher convened there on Monday. Suspicion quickly settled on Newton Bateman, sixteen-year-old son of Thomas Bateman, who had been seen in the vicinity of the crime near the time it occurred. Twenty-two-year-old Harry Knappenberger told the jury that, after he saw the McLaughlin girls pass his house about 3:00 p.m. Sunday, he started along the same road several minutes later, and Newton Bateman quickly overtook him. They walked together a short distance, until they came to the first bend in the road, at which point young Bateman took another lane, saying he was going to his uncle's house, while Knappenberger continued on toward Flag Springs.

Newton Bateman was briefly detained and questioned on Monday but was released later the same day after he told the jury he didn't even own a gun. However, the investigation continued to focus on the Bateman family. Among the witnesses interviewed by the coroner's jury was Newton's eighteen-year-old sister, Elizabeth, who said her older brother, twenty-two-year-old Oliver, was home all afternoon on Sunday, but she was unable to offer an airtight alibi for Newton. Two other young girls of the neighborhood testified that Newton Bateman had once tried to lure them into the same cornfield where the McLaughlin girls' bodies were found. Another witness swore, in contradiction to what Newton had told the jury, that he had recently sold young Bateman a pistol, and others said they thought Newton or his family owned at least two revolvers.

Austie and Adella McLaughlin were buried on Tuesday, September 2, at the Flag Springs Baptist Cemetery with hundreds of people in attendance. Over $150 was pledged by the people present to purchase monuments for the little girls.

Meanwhile, the coroner's investigation continued. On Tuesday, Booher went to the Bateman home, and as he approached, he saw the mother, Mary Bateman, hurry out the back door to the woodshed and throw something under a box. After she emerged, Booher went into the shed and found a box of cartridges. He then demanded that the two revolvers Newton Bateman was thought to have in his possession be turned over, and Mrs. Bateman readily handed one of them over. After much negotiating, Booher finally convinced her to give up the other one as well, and she retrieved it from its hiding place, buried behind the house near a cherry tree. One of the chambers of the weapon, a double-barrel pistol, corresponded with the .32 bullet that had been found in Austie McLaughlin's head.

The question that now faced the jury, Prosecutor Booher told a newspaper reporter, was

> whether Newton Bateman went on to his uncle's as he stated..., whether he turned into the woods and cornfield and intersected the girls, whether Harry Knappenberger knows anything about it, whether the girls had been killed before Harry passed to the road..., or whether Oliver Bateman, who was left at home, cut across the pasture and south cornfield and killed the girls before Harry and Newton came near.

Newton Bateman was re-arrested on Wednesday, and Oliver Bateman also came under renewed suspicion when a boot print found near the scene of the murders was found to be a perfect fit to a pair of boots he owned. However, a few on the jury felt the case against either Bateman was based on thin circumstantial evidence, and they believed the murders had been committed by "a tramp" passing through the area rather than by someone from the neighborhood. Unable to agree entirely, the jury finally reached a verdict late Wednesday night or Thursday morning that the McLaughlin girls had come to their death at the hands of a party or parties unknown.

Despite the verdict, the investigation continued, and the Batemans remained the primary focus. On Friday the 5th, the inquiry took a dramatic turn that pointed to the last of Prosecutor Booher's possible explanations of the murders as the most likely scenario. A shirt with a bloodstain that someone had tried to wash out was found at the Bateman home, and it was identified as belonging to Oliver Bateman. The suspect's sister, Elizabeth, then recanted her testimony that Oliver had been home all day Sunday, saying instead that he left home about 2:00 p.m. and did not return until about 5:00 p.m.

Oliver Bateman, who had been lying at home for the past several days claiming to be sick, was immediately arrested. Still protesting his innocence, he was taken to Savannah and lodged in the Andrew County Jail.

Prosecutor Booher and Andrew County sheriff John Lincoln kept gathering evidence against Bateman after he was placed in jail. On Monday morning, September 8, they had the body of Austie McLaughlin exhumed, and a post mortem examination revealed that what had previously been thought to be an abrasion was actually a second bullet hole. A .22 caliber bullet found in the body matched the second barrel of the revolver that had been hidden behind the Bateman home and recovered by Booher.

Presented with this additional evidence, Oliver Bateman broke down and gave a full confession. At least two different versions of the confession were published in newspapers at the time. It's possible Bateman gave two entirely separate statements, but more likely the different versions merely represent different transcriptions of the same statement. The following account is based largely on the confession as it appeared in the *Holt County Sentinel* six days after the statement was made.

Bateman said he got some liquor from a stranger and had been drinking on Sunday, August 31. He said he left his house about fifteen minutes after the McLaughlin girls did with no intention of hurting them, because he had no ill feeling toward them and even liked them and considered them friends. However, when he spotted them near the Knappenberger place, he decided to follow them but even then with no real intent to do them harm. He overtook them at the cornfield where they were gathering hazelnuts. Climbing over the fence to talk to them, he lured them deeper into the field, where he made indecent sexual proposals to the older girl.

Austie rebuffed him "in a most indignant manner," and started back toward the road with her little sister alongside and Bateman following. Angered by the rejection, Bateman decided to kill the nine-year-old girl, and he shot her in the body with the .22 barrel of his pistol. When she turned to face him, he shot her in the head with the .32 shot, killing her almost instantly. Little Adella started running, but he chased after her and caught her. She begged him to let her go, promising not to tell anyone, and he momentarily released her. She cried and yelled as she ran away, and, knowing she would tell on him, he caught her again, threw her down, and sliced her throat.

After killing the younger girl, Bateman said, he went back to the nine-year-old, took off her clothes, and "outraged her, cutting a place with my knife large enough to make an entrance." Afterward, he disemboweled her to create an impression the deed had been done by a madman. He then went back to the littler girl and moved her body into the weeds.

Bateman saw Harry Knappenberger on the road next to the cornfield and waited for him to pass. Then he crossed the road and went through a pasture to a creek, where he washed his hands and threw the knife into the water. He went home, washed the blood out of his shirt, and lay it out to dry.

He said he didn't know what possessed him to kill the girls other than the whiskey he drank. "I do not want to live, nor do I expect to," he concluded. "What I have done deserves death." He was ready to die at that very moment. The sooner, the better, he said.

Another version of Bateman's confession, drawn from contemporaneous accounts in the *Savannah Democrat* and/or the *Savannah Reporter*, appears in the 1888 *History of Andrew and DeKalb Counties*. It differs in several respects from the *Sentinel* account cited above. In the county history version, Bateman said that, after seeing the girls near the Knappenberger place, he cut across a pasture straight to Dr. Lockett's cornfield rather than following the girls along the road to the cornfield. He said he killed them fifteen or twenty minutes after Harry Knappenberger had passed the cornfield rather than before Harry passed. The county history version does not mention Bateman having made indecent proposals to Austie McLaughlin and offers no possible motive for the killings. The county history version does state, however, that Bateman said he had never had sexual intercourse with a woman, a detail omitted from the *Sentinel* transcription. The county history account also adds to the *Sentinel* story that Bateman lay down when he got home after killing the girls, telling his sister to wake him if anybody came. When Ira McLaughlin called about sundown looking for his sisters, Bateman said he wanted to help hunt for them but that his parents wouldn't let him because they thought he was sick. Contrary to the *Sentinel* version, which makes repeated references to Bateman's intoxication as a reason for his action, the county history version mentions his drinking excuse only to discount it.

Indeed, Bateman's parents were said to have denied that their son had been drinking when they heard that he had offered it as an excuse for his heinous deeds. The general belief among the people around Flag Springs was that Bateman had invented the whiskey aspect of his story as a lie to try to mitigate his guilt. Other inconsistencies in his story also called its veracity into question. In both published versions of his story, for instance, he said that he threw the knife with which he'd killed Adella McLaughlin in the creek. However, he later wrote to an acquaintance in the Flag Springs area that the knife was hidden in the kitchen loft of the Bateman home, and several men went to the home and found it where the letter said it was.

The people grew incensed upon learning the lurid details of Bateman's confession, and there was excited talk of mob action on Monday night the 8th. Fearing a lynching, Sheriff Lincoln secretly took the prisoner to St. Joseph about midnight, but the secret didn't stay hidden very long. On the night of September 9, a crowd gathered around the jail at St. Joe, and Lincoln, assisted by the Buchanan County sheriff, once again slipped away with his prisoner and brought him back to Savannah.

Still insisting that he was ready to die, Bateman asked that a special term of circuit court be called so that he could plead guilty as soon as possible, and Judge Henry Kelley granted the request, setting Thursday, October 2, for the opening date of the trial. On that day, a grand jury handed down two indictments for murder against Bateman, who refused the judge's offer to appoint an attorney to defend him. Kelley presented the indictments to the defendant and then adjourned until Monday morning, giving Bateman time to study the charges and reflect on his intent to plead guilty. As he was led from the courtroom back to jail, Bateman's only comment was that he wished the matter had been settled that very day. He repeated that he was guilty and was ready to die.

On Monday morning the 6th, a large crowd gathered in Savannah for Bateman's trial, and it was whispered about that he had changed his mind and was now ready to plead not guilty. The rumor aroused the people to renewed threats of lynching in case the gossip should prove true, but they needn't have worried.

When Judge Kelley finally called the court to order

Monday afternoon, Bateman said he was ready to plead. Prosecutor Booher read the indictments, and Bateman pled guilty in an even, impassive voice. Kelley then sentenced him to be hanged by the neck until dead on November 21, 1884, between the hours of 10:00 a.m. and 4:00 p.m. Again, Bateman's only objection was that he couldn't die that very day but instead had to wait a month and a half.

During the interval, Bateman continued to insist that he was ready to die and only wished that the appointed day would hurry up and arrive, and he was watched closely to prevent a possible suicide. The prisoner entertained a host of visitors in his cell, including not only spiritual advisors and members of his family but also members of the press from far and wide, who were eager to relate his shocking story.

On November 20, he was visited by three ministers, and he professed religion. But he would never state why he had killed the little girls other than to say the idea had suddenly come upon him when he'd seen them in the cornfield. Curious observers were left with vague speculations like those of a doctor who interviewed Bateman and concluded that he was motivated to kill the girls by "a low order of instinctive desire through animal lust."

Bateman reportedly slept soundly on the night of November 20 and awoke early the next morning, greeting his last day on earth in a cheerful mood. He ate a hearty breakfast, but when newspapermen from Kansas City, St. Louis, and other cities tried to visit him in his cell, Bateman said he had told everything there was to tell and didn't have anything left to say.

A crowd had started forming in Savannah the previous day, and people continued to pour in during the night and the early morning of the 21st until there were close to 10,000 spectators in Savannah, eager to witness Oliver Bateman's hanging.

At mid-morning, Bateman was visited by his father and then by two of the same ministers who'd seen him the day before. At noon, Sheriff Lincoln read the death warrant to the condemned man. A half hour later, Bateman was placed in a carriage and driven to the scaffold that had been erected at the edge of town. He ascended the stairs with a firm step and walked unhesitantly to the trap, where the rope was adjusted around his neck. One of the preachers offered a final prayer, a black cap was drawn over Bateman's face, and then Sheriff Lincoln sprung the trap, swinging the villain into eternity at exactly 12:55 p.m. on November 21, 1884. He was declared dead eight minutes later, and his body was cut down after another half hour.

EXPIATION.

Bateman, the Brutal and Bloody Butcher, Hanged at Savannah.

A Throng of Ten Thousand Witnessed the Terrible Trapeze Act.

As He Lived, So Died, the Blackest Criminal on Record.

He Meets His Fate with Stoical and Cool Indifference.

The Monstrous Murder of the McLaughlin Girls Expiated.

THE EXECUTION.

Sedalia Weekly Bazoo describes Bateman's "terrible trapeze act."

The body was placed in a coffin. Thomas Bateman, who'd stayed uptown rather than witness the horrid scene, took charge of the body and buried his son on the Bateman farm near Flag Springs.

But that was not quite the end of the story.   On January 17, 1885, a St. Joseph correspondent wrote to the *St. Louis Missouri Republican* declaring that the mystery of why Oliver Bateman had killed the McLaughlin girls had been solved. Oliver Bateman's sister Elizabeth had turned up pregnant since the murders, and it had come out that Oliver had been carrying on an incestuous affair with her since at least June 15, 1884, when the two had been discovered having carnal relations in an outhouse on their father's farm. According to neighbors of the Batemans to whom the correspondent had talked, when the McLaughlin girls had visited the Bateman home on August 31, they had found only Oliver and his sister at the house by themselves, and they had witnessed Oliver "fondling and caressing his sister and manifesting lustful passions" toward her. Oliver had killed the girls to keep them from telling what they had seen. The *Republican* published the correspondent's allegations the next day, January 18, under the headline "Cause of a Double Murder."

The Batemans subsequently sued the newspaper for libel and won an award of $5,000 in the St. Louis City Circuit Court. The newspaper appealed to the Missouri Supreme Court, and the high court overruled the lower court's verdict, saying that, since this was a civil case, the newspaper did not have to prove its allegations beyond a reasonable doubt as long as a preponderance of evidence showed them to be true.

11

A Red-Handed Desperado

The Lynching of Omaha Charley

Throughout Missouri's history, Nodaway County has distinguished itself in the business of lynching. Many readers may be familiar with the vigilante killing of town bully Ken McElroy by gunfire in broad daylight on the streets of Skidmore in July 1981, which is sometimes cited as Missouri's last lynching. Almost as well known and sensational as the McElroy case is that of Raymond Gunn, a black man who was burned to death by a mob in the county seat of Maryville in 1931 after he allegedly raped and killed a young white schoolteacher. But Nodaway County's dubious lineage of extralegal executions stretches back even farther, at least to 1884, when the notorious Omaha Charley was hanged by a mob in Maryville.

Sometime after 1870, Charles Stephens left his native state of Kentucky and traveled around Iowa and Nebraska a few years before coming to Missouri and landing in Maryville around early May of 1878 when he was about thirty-five years old. Dubbed Omaha Charley because of his previous residence, he spent his time gambling and hanging around saloons. He was rumored to have previously killed a man and was considered a desperate character.

He took a job working in Jake Schroeder's saloon and was tending bar there when Jake Layton and John Mahan came in together about 6:00 p.m., March 1, 1879. Layton was drinking at the bar and conversing across the counter with Charley when the two got into a quarrel over a woman, and Charley ordered the customer to leave. Layton refused, and Charley started around the bar. When he saw Layton coming, he fired an errant shot, and Mahan grabbed him, presumably to keep him from firing at Layton again. Stephens then shot Mahan three times, mortally wounding him.

Stephens was arrested and lodged in jail to await trial. At the June 1879 term of Nodaway County Circuit Court, he was found guilty of second degree murder. Sentenced to twelve years in the state penitentiary, he was received at the Jefferson City facility on July 15, 1879. He was pardoned, however, by Missouri governor Thomas Crittenden, on January 1, 1884, after serving less than half his term. Crittenden reportedly took the action to fulfill a promise he'd made to his deceased daughter, Carrie. Stricken with a deadly case of diphtheria, the little girl had taken a liking to Omaha Charley after he fashioned a number of handmade trinkets for her, and she asked her father to set him free if she died.

However, the romantic circumstances surrounding Omaha Charley's early release little swayed the people of Maryville in their opinion of the ex-con. When Stephens showed back up in their community in early 1884 and resumed his old lifestyle, the citizens greeted his reappearance and the governor's leniency with equal disgust.

According to a later report in the *St. Louis Post-Dispatch*, Omaha Charley

> frequented saloons during the day, and at night ran a secret gambling den, where the vilest characters met and prolonged their nocturnal debauches. His bearing was even more reckless than before his incarceration.... It was quite a common remark about town that it was only a question of time when "Omaha Charley" could add another to his list of murders.

Omaha Charley took time out from his revelry to get married in late 1884, but the hiatus proved brief. The feared prophecy that he might kill another man came true, or nearly so, on the night of Wednesday, December 3, 1884, just a few days after his marriage. Omaha Charley entered Michael Hilgert's saloon in a state of intoxication and insulted the first few men he saw, but knowing the desperate character of the troublemaker, they retreated from a confrontation.

Stephens then walked up to the bar, where Herbert Kremer, a former resident of Maryville who'd recently returned for a visit, stood with several friends. Omaha Charley ordered a shot of liquor and promptly spilled part of it on Kremer's coat (intentionally, according to some reports). When Kremer told him to be more careful, Stephens replied that perhaps Kremer would like the rest of the drink in his face. Kremer said "No," but Omaha Charley retorted that he guessed he'd give it to him anyway. He threw the liquor in Kremer's face, and immediately drew a revolver and shot the man in the breast.

Despite being shot, Kremer, according to one report, knocked Stephens to the floor and "beat him into a state of insensibility." Officers arrived shortly afterward, arrested Omaha Charley, and locked him in the Nodaway County Jail. Although Kremer was able to walk to a doctor's office under his own power, his wound was thought fatal at first, and sentiment against Omaha Charley ran high. Few citizens talked openly of a lynching, but many discussed the probability that Stephens might escape punishment through the interference of Governor Crittenden.

And some were plotting in secret. Despite the fact that Kremer was improving and was now given a fair chance of recovery, those inclined to take the law into their own hands decided to put their vigilante plan into action late on the night of Monday, December 8. About twenty or thirty masked men formed at the fairgrounds at the east edge of Maryville about midnight and started uptown about 12:30 Tuesday morning.

Arriving at the jail about 1:00 a.m., the vigilantes knocked on the door of the building that housed both the jail and the upstairs quarters of Sheriff James Anderson. When Anderson refused their demand that he open the outside door, they promptly started knocking it down. When they broke through, both the sheriff and his brother, Jack Anderson, who was also a deputy, opened fire, wounding one of the vigilantes, but the would-be lynchers returned fire and gained entrance. Anderson and his brother, out of ammunition, retreated to an upstairs landing, where they were pursued and overpowered by the mob before they could reload.

Commandeering the keys from the sheriff, the vigilantes went downstairs and opened Omaha Charley's cell door. Stephens fought like a madman, but the mob dragged him outside and placed a rope around his neck. They half-carried and half-dragged the prisoner to a bridge about four blocks east of the jail on Fourth Street and fixed the other end of the rope to the bridge's railing.

Omaha Charley asked the masked men whether they weren't at least going to let him say something, and they gave him a chance to say his piece. "Gentlemen, what is all this about?" he demanded.

The lynchers asked him if that was all he had to say, and when he did not reply promptly, they shoved him over the bridge. He clung momentarily to the railing before losing his grip.

"My God!" he screamed as he dropped. He fell about eight feet before the rope caught and jerked him into the hereafter. His neck broke at the first drop, but to be sure he was dead, the mob drew him back up and let him fall again. Now satisfied, the lynchers marched off into the night, leaving the body of Omaha Charley swaying in the moonlight.

The sheriff was notified of the lynching, and after an hour or two, the body was cut down and taken back into town, where an inquest was held later the same day. Despite the fact that one of the vigilantes had suffered a fairly serious gunshot wound, little effort was made to ascertain his identity or that of any of his cohorts. After interviewing the sheriff, his brother, and a couple of bystanders who had trailed the lynch party toward the hanging bridge, the coroner's jury concluded that Stephens had come to his death by the usual means—"at the hands of divers parties unknown to this jury."

OMAHA CHARLIE.

Charles Stevens Pays the Penalty of
his Many Misdeeds.

Maryville Mob Swings Him from the
Railway Bridge.

Charley's Last Words—His Fight with
his Assailants.

With   Benefit of Clergy, he is
Hurled into Eternity.

Gallant Defense by the Sheriff and his
Deputy.

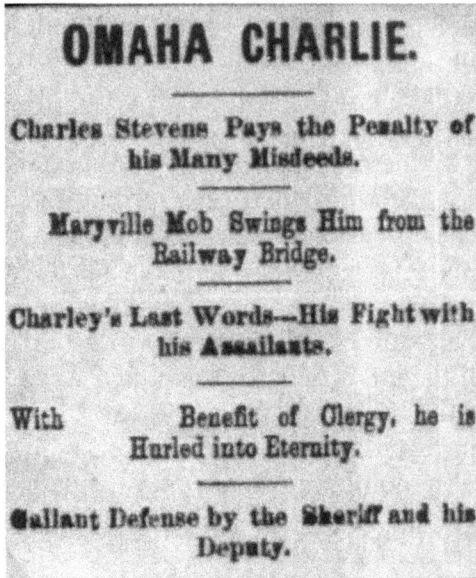

Headline from *St. Joseph Weekly Herald* tells of Omaha Charley's demise.

At mid-afternoon on December 9, Omaha Charley's body was turned over to a local undertaker, and hundreds of curious spectators came by to view the body. Later the same day, the corpse was taken to a potter's field, with Annabelle Swinford, Stephens's recently wedded wife, trailing the burial party.

After Omaha Charley's lynching, rumors circulated around Maryville that Annabelle planned to sue the county over the mob action, but nothing ever came of her threat.

L. M. Lane, Nodaway County prosecuting attorney, wrote to Governor Crittenden the day after Stephens's lynching asking the state's help in apprehending the men who took the law into their own hands. Specifically, the prosecutor suggested that Crittenden might offer a reward as an incentive for witnesses against the mob to come forward.

The governor replied a few days later declining to offer a reward for what he thought should be a matter of civic duty. Crittenden reminded Lane that the citizens of his neighboring county of Andrew had refrained from vigilantism against Oliver Bateman even in the face of a much more heinous crime than Omaha Charley's, and the governor severely chastised not only the Nodaway vigilantes for their cowardly act of taking an unarmed man from jail and executing him before he had even been tried in a court of law but also the officials and citizens who stood by and let it happen. Crittenden told Lane that he should be able to adequately prosecute the case against the lynchers without the aid of the state.

Editorial critique of Governor Crittenden's letter to Lane was swift and harsh. The *St. Louis Post-Dispatch*, for example, blasted the governor for his "stereotyped and orthodox homily against lynching." Noting Crittenden's accusation that vigilante acts like the lynching of Stephens breed contempt for the law, the *Post-Dispatch* countered that, in order for a lynching to occur, contempt for the law must exist long before the act happens. The newspaper concluded:

> And, unfortunately, this Nodaway case is one in which contempt for the courts of law began with the Governor himself and emanated from him to the people. He set the example of treating the juries and courts of Nodaway County with contempt when he pardoned this red-handed desperado, "Omaha Charley," out of the penitentiary. A Governor so notorious for gross abuse of the pardoning power is not the proper person to lecture the Nodaway people on submission to the decisions of the courts.

12

The Damned Thing Has Got to Be Rid Of

Murder of the Hall Family and Hanging of Joseph Howell

Joseph A. Howell maintained at his 1889 trial for the murder of his cousin Malinda "Minnie" Hall and her four kids that his relations with Minnie were pleasant and friendly but in no way improper and that he thought of her as a sister. One of Howell's best friends, Henry Smith, testified, on the other hand, that he overheard Minnie tell Howell just three weeks before her death that Howell was the only one except her deceased husband who'd ever "meddled with" her. Smith added that Howell had later confessed to him that Minnie was pregnant, that she told Howell he was the father, and that Howell had vowed to get rid of the unborn child. One of the young men was lying, and almost nobody thought it was Henry Smith. It took four and a half years, though, before Howell finally paid the ultimate price for his heinous crime.

About half past ten o'clock on the night of Saturday, January 19, 1889, Minnie Hall's home in rural Linn County about five miles southwest of Brookfield, Missouri, was discovered on fire, and R. N. Vorce and other neighbors who rushed to the scene found the structure almost completely engulfed when they arrived. Vorce saw the lifeless bodies of Minnie Hall and her five-year-old daughter, Nettie, inside the burning structure, but only Nettie could be pulled from the blaze before the house collapsed. Although she was dead, the body was not burned beyond recognition, and it was positively identified as that of Nettie Hall. After the fire died down, four other bodies were retrieved from the smoldering rubble. Although they could not positively be identified, one was almost certainly Minnie Hall, since Vorce had seen her inside the burning structure before it gave way. The other three were presumed to be Nettie's siblings; nine-year-old Willie, seven-year-old May, and two-year-old Roy.

Scattered hay and footprints leading to and from a nearby haystack were seen in the fresh snow that had fallen that evening. Upon further inspection, the neighbors concluded that hay had been taken from the stack and placed under the house to fuel the blaze.

Footprints of the person who'd set the fire led away from the Hall property toward Brookfield, and four young men were detailed about midnight to follow the trail and try to arrest the arsonist. The four men followed the footprints to Brookfield, where two of the posse went to the train depot to inquire about departures and to enlist the cooperation of railroad officials in capturing the fugitive. The other two followed the trail to the Clark Hotel in downtown Brookfield. One of these two stayed at the hotel while the other left to enlist City Marshal Critchfield's help. Joining the search, Critchfield and his two ad hoc deputies picked up the track but momentarily lost it before coming upon some railroad officials and other parties who had spotted a fleeing man they thought was the fugitive. Critchfield rejoined the pursuit through the streets but again lost track of his man near the Babb Hotel. The marshal went inside the hotel and was informed that a man signing his name as J. A. Howell had just checked in minutes before.

Critchfield found Howell in an upstairs room and placed him under arrest about three o'clock on the morning of the 20th. When Howell asked what the problem was, the marshal told him a woman and four children had been burned up in a house fire and the track of the arsonist had been followed to this hotel. Howell responded that he hadn't been out in the country tonight, even though Critchfield had not told him where the fire was. The suspect's pant legs were wet, as if from tramping through tall, snow-covered grass. The tread of his overshoes appeared to match the tracks that had been followed from the fire, and a search of his clothing turned up some matches and a pistol that seemed to have been recently fired.

Joseph A. Howell from the *Trenton Evening Republican*.

Twenty-four-year-old Joseph A. Howell had come to Missouri in the fall of 1886 from his home state of Ohio. He met Henry Smith in St. Louis, and they traveled to Memphis and other places together before coming to Kansas City. In the spring of 1887, Howell and Smith moved to the Linn County area, where Howell had relatives. He stayed at first in neighboring Chariton County with his aunt Sarah Brooks, who was Minnie's mother, while Smith began working on R. N. Vorce's farm less than a mile from Minnie. After staying with Mrs. Brooks a few days, Howell came to Minnie's house and stayed with her and her husband, Ansel, for about a week. He then lived with Ansel's father, James Hall, working as a farmhand, throughout the spring and summer of 1887. From there he went to a neighbor of the Halls and continued as a farmhand until he took a teaching job at Prairie Mound for the 1888-1889 school year.

Ansel had died in the meantime, and Howell started paying regular visits to the thirty-one-year-old widow and her kids about the time school began. He boarded at the school during the week but often spent the weekend with Minnie, whose house was about five miles northeast of Prairie Mound, midway to Brookfield. He might have looked upon her as a sister at first, but they quickly became kissing cousins and then some.

And now he was accused of killing her.

After daylight on Sunday morning, a coroner's inquest was held at the scene of the crime. The charred bodies of the victims were closely examined, and it appeared their skulls had been split open with a hatchet or other sharp instrument. In the cellar beneath the burnt house a human fetus about six or seven months old was discovered. The fetus had been buried in the dirt floor of the cellar prior to the fire and had escaped serious defacement. A broken chamber pot, in which it was thought the fetus had been carried, was found a few feet away on the floor of the cellar. The only entrance to the cellar was from the exterior of the house, and the door had been taken off and laid aside. When investigators lifted it up, they saw snow on the ground where the door had lain, showing that it had been removed after it started snowing early Saturday evening. The coroner's jury concluded that Howell had induced an abortion on Minnie, and, when it looked as though she would not survive the procedure, he had killed her and her children and burned their bodies to cover up the first crime.

Excitement ran high in Brookfield as word of the brutal crime spread, and "almost everybody thought Howell should be hung at once," according to one report. For safekeeping, Howell was taken to the Linn County Jail at Linneus on Sunday afternoon. He was supposed to be brought back to Brookfield for his preliminary hearing within a day or two, but a mob of about 200 people formed there on both Monday and Tuesday in anticipation of the proceeding, and it was postponed.

The remains of Minnie Hall and her children were buried on Monday. Initial reports said they were buried in a common grave. Perhaps they were, but today they have separate markers at Rose Hill Cemetery in Brookfield beside Ansel Hall's grave.

After the angry cries for vigilante justice died down, Howell was indicted for first-degree murder in the deaths of all five victims, but prosecutors chose to try him only for the murder of Nettie Hall, since her body was the one that could be definitely identified. His trial began at Linneus in late July of 1889.

Most of the forty-plus witnesses at the trial testified for the prosecution. These included neighbors who discovered the fire and pulled the bodies from the burned home, the men involved in tracking Howell to the Babb Hotel, Marshal Critchfield, and members of the coroner's jury. Perhaps the most damning witness, though, was Henry Smith, because his testimony clearly established motive.

Smith said that, three or four weeks before the murder, Howell asked him to accompany him on a visit to Minnie's house, because there were rumors about him and his cousin and he did not want to go there alone. After they arrived, Smith overheard Howell and Minnie arguing. She threatened to tell James Hall, although Smith did not know then what the threat was about, and Howell replied, "Tell him and be damned."

Minnie then told Howell that no one except him and her deceased husband had ever "meddled with" (i.e. had sexual intercourse with) her. Howell didn't believe her and said there were "other parties running after" her.

After Smith and Howell left Minnie's, Howell confessed that Minnie was pregnant and that she claimed Howell was the father. Seeming to admit that he was indeed the father, Howell told Smith he would marry Minnie if she were "a nice woman," but he didn't think he was the only one who had been "running there."

Smith advised his friend to just leave the territory, but Howell said he had a reputation to uphold and couldn't let Minnie's unborn child wreck it. Saying "the damned thing has got to be rid of," he asked Smith if he knew any doctor from whom he might procure a drug to induce an abortion.

Howell's lawyers tried to impeach Smith's testimony by suggesting that the witness might have been "meddling with" Minnie Hall himself. However, Smith had an ironclad alibi, because he was at Vorce's farm when the crime was committed.

The main defense strategy was to try to set up an alibi. Taking the stand himself, Howell admitted having visited Minnie's house during the mid-afternoon on the Saturday of the crime, but he said he came to Brookfield about suppertime and stayed there until he was arrested in the wee hours of Sunday morning. He denied virtually all of Henry Smith's testimony, and he also said he was not the man chased through Brookfield's streets.

Several witnesses vouched that they'd seen Howell in Brookfield as late as eight p.m. on the night in question, and one said he saw the defendant in town even later than that. Howell's lawyers argued that their client could not possibly have had time to walk to Minnie's, abort the baby, kill the family, and set the fire during the interval between the time Howell was last seen in Brookfield and the time the fire was discovered. The prosecution countered that the abortifacient was likely administered during the defendant's afternoon visit to the Hall home and that, when he returned for his second visit, he found Minnie in a violent or dying agony and committed the murders almost immediately.

Several witnesses also testified to Howell's good character, including at least one or two who'd known him in Ohio.

The trial ended on July 27, 1889. After deliberating about an hour, the jury found Howell guilty of first-degree murder, and a few days later he was sentenced to hang. His lawyers appealed the verdict to the Missouri Supreme Court, however, and the execution was postponed pending the outcome of the appeal.

The appeal was sustained at the April 1890 term of the Missouri Supreme Court. The justices ruled that the lower court had erred in its instructions to the jury, and the case was remanded to the Linn County Circuit Court for retrial.

The case was scheduled to be reheard in the fall of 1890, but Howell asked for and was granted a change of venue to Grundy County, citing the prejudice that existed against him in the Linn-Chariton county area.

Howell's second trial began at Trenton in late April 1891. In early May, the jury announced that they were hopelessly split (reportedly 9 to 3 in favor of conviction), and a mistrial was declared.

A third trial was set for the August term of the Grundy County Circuit Court but didn't come off until early October. About the only significant new piece of evidence introduced that had not been presented at the first trial was a purported confession Howell had made to two cellmates while he was still being held at Linneus. Howell supposedly said that, when he got to Minnie's house and found her already almost dead, he picked up an ax and finished her off.

He started to leave, but Minnie's older boy started crying and hid behind some barrels. Howell reached over the barrels and knocked the boy's brains out. By now, the little girls were screaming, too, and the murderer brained them and the little boy as well.

The trial concluded on October 9, when the jury, after deliberating about an hour and half, declared the defendant guilty of first-degree murder in the case of Nettie Hall. Howell showed no emotion when the verdict was given, according to the *Macon Times*, but did curse the jurors and even his own attorneys as he was led back to jail. The *Times* said of the prisoner at the time, "Howell has rather a good looking face, front view, but a side view will reveal a licentious chin, turned outward sufficiently for a gourd handle. The back of his head bulges largely and is covered with a growth of thick, coarse, reddish hair."

Judge Charles Goodman gave Howell's attorneys until Monday, October 26 to file a motion for a new trial. The court convened on that date, and the hearing lasted until Tuesday night. On Wednesday morning the judge rendered his decision denying the motion. Ordering Howell to stand, Goodman then pronounced a death sentence on him, fixing December 18, 1891, as the date of the hanging.

Howell's lawyers immediately filed an appeal, and the execution was stayed, pending the outcome. For the second time, Howell's case was referred to the Missouri Supreme Court, but the bill of exceptions filed by his attorneys did not reach Jefferson City until January 1893. The case was finally argued before the high court at the April 1893 term, but shortly thereafter the state discovered that the bill of exceptions had not contained an accurate transcript of the evidence. The defense lawyers had tampered with some of the records after Judge Goodman signed the bill of exceptions so that it appeared the body of Nettie Hall had never been positively identified. The Grundy County Circuit Court was ordered to forward a true transcript of the case forthwith.

On June 27, the Missouri Supreme Court sustained the lower court's guilty verdict and set August 4 as the execution date. Howell's lawyers were strongly censured, and two of them were later disbarred over the "mutilated records case."

As Howell's date with death approached, he met with his spiritual advisors regularly and expressed a belief in the hereafter but professed no particular religion. Still maintaining his innocence, he said that any purported statements he'd made to the contrary were lies concocted by others.

A scaffold was erected inside a stockade at the Grundy County courthouse in Trenton, and Howell was led to the gallows about ten o'clock Friday morning, August 4, 1893. Although emaciated by his four and a half years in confinement, the condemned man "seemed cool," according to the *Brookfield Gazette*, and the deputies who bound his hands and feet "were more nervous than the prisoner." Howell dropped through the trap at exactly 10:12 a.m. and was pronounced dead eight minutes later. Among a select group of spectators allowed inside the stockade to watch Howell die was A. J. Brooks, Minnie Hall's father.

After Howell's body was cut down, it was taken to the courtyard, where thousands of curious onlookers were allowed to gawk at it. In accordance with Howell's wishes, he was buried at Trenton's Maple Grove Cemetery in a ceremony witnessed by about 5,000 people.

13

A Professional Butcher

Slaughters His Own Family

Bates Soper Expiates His Carnage on the Gallows

After John L. Soper was shot and killed on his farm near Kearney, Missouri, in March of 1880, a "terrible suspicion" prevailed that he'd been murdered by his own son, Bates Soper. The suspicion that rested on Bates created bitter conflict in the Soper family, and one of his brothers reportedly even threatened to kill Bates on sight if he didn't stay away from him.

But there was not enough evidence against the twenty-five-year-old Soper to arrest him for killing his father. In fact, another man was soon arrested instead, although he, too, was later released for lack of evidence.

Bates couldn't stay out of trouble, though. About the same time as his father's death, Soper stole a horse and was arrested shortly afterward. Convicted of grand larceny at the February 1881 term of Clay County Circuit Court, he was sentenced to two years in the Missouri State Penitentiary and was transferred to Jefferson City on March 19. He managed to behave himself well enough during his incarceration to warrant a discharge on September 19, 1882, under the state's three-fourths law, which allowed for early release for good conduct.

After his release, Soper wasted little time before launching into a romance with twenty-five-year-old Delia Hunt. It's likely the couple might have known each other before Bates was sent to prison, since he grew up in the Kearney vicinity of Clay County and she lived in neighboring Clinton County. In fact, their marriage in late January of 1883, four months after his release from prison, took place in Clinton County but was recorded in Clay County.

The couple lived with Soper's mother in Clay County for six years after their marriage. They then moved to the Fayetteville, Arkansas, area for about a year and a half. In 1890, the family, now consisting of two small children in addition to the father and mother, came to Archie, Missouri, where Soper went into business as a butcher.

Neighbors of the Sopers were accustomed to seeing Delia Soper working about her house and her two children playing in the yard, and they became concerned after several days passed in late April of 1891 with no sign of the family. Knocks on the door went unanswered, and none of the neighbors had heard of any plans for the Sopers to be away from home. After a couple of days, one of the neighbors also noticed a swarm of flies hovering near the house. Late Friday afternoon, April 24, the Archie city marshal was summoned, and he and several citizens went to the Soper home and broke into the east room.

What they found was a horrifying spectacle.

On the floor in the middle of the room lay the body of the Sopers' daughter, six-year-old Maude. The "sunny-haired" little girl had her skull broken and her brains spattered upon the floor beside her. She had apparently been hit by an ax and then "repeatedly struck and mashed by the fiend" after she fell.

The door to the next room was open, and when the investigating party stepped through, the scene that met their eyes was just as sickening as the one in the first room. Delia Soper lay sprawled on the floor with her face "pounded to a jelly and her skull pounded to a shapeless mass, with brains matting the hair low over the sockets where eyes…once pleaded for life." By the mother's side lay the little boy, three-year-old Gillis, with his head split open but otherwise not battered and mutilated like those of his mother and sister.

In a corner of one room stood a bloodstained ax with

clumps of hair matted to the dry blood. Two notes were found on a table in the mother and son's room, and they appeared to be in the handwriting of Bates Soper. In the notes, one of which he asked to be delivered to the *Kansas City Times*, he virtually admitted the grisly murders, saying his family was better off dead than suffering through a miserable life as he had. He said he was going to Clay County to kill the devil who had caused all his problems and that he was then going to kill himself.

Further investigation revealed that Soper had, indeed, bought a train ticket in Archie bound for Kansas City early on Wednesday morning, shortly after the presumed time of the murders. But there was no trace of him in neighboring Clay County. Instead of continuing on to his home territory to kill "the devil," Soper had simply disappeared.

Six years passed with no sign of the fugitive nor word of his whereabouts. A reward of $700 was offered for Soper's arrest, and Kansas City detective Samuel E. Lowe took up the case. He ran down several fruitless leads before his brother, Jackson County prosecuting attorney Frank M. Lowe, saw a notice in an Oregon newspaper in the spring of 1897 about a man named Sandy Soper, who had abandoned his wife in Portland, taking their two-year-old son with him.

Detective Lowe's inquiries led him to believe that the wife deserter was likely the same man who was wanted for killing his first family six years earlier. Armed with requisition papers from the Missouri governor, Lowe set out for the West Coast about the first of June. He tracked Sandy Soper to Ashland, Oregon, where he found him working in an orchard south of town on June 9, 1897, under the name of Homer Lee. The fugitive, though, admitted his true identity as soon as he was placed under arrest, and he offered no resistance.

Soper spent the night of the 9th in a local jail, and an Ashland newspaperman visited him in the clink. The reporter described Soper as being of "low stature" and weighing probably not over 130 pounds. "He is sandy complexioned, his mustache and hair being decidedly reddish."

Detective Lowe escorted Soper back to Kansas City, where they were met by Frank Lowe on the evening of June 15. The two brothers took the prisoner immediately to Harrisonville and lodged him in the Cass County Jail to await trial.

Conjecture abounded at the time of Soper's arrest that he might have also killed his two-year-old son, just as he had his first family, and shortly after he got back to Missouri, the prisoner made a full confession confirming the suspicion. He said that he left his Portland wife and home on April 16, 1891, taking the child with him. Since he was going away, he didn't want his son to live; so he tossed the boy in the Willamette River, watched him drown, and then hid the body in Montgomery Gulch on Portland's east side. The body was found about the first of July, based on Soper's description of where he had hidden it.

Soper also freely confessed his guilt in the 1891 murders at Archie, although he offered few additional details at first. A report from Harrisonville, published in area newspapers shortly after Soper confessed to the murder of his Oregon son, noted that the prisoner "seems to feel little or no remorse for any of his crimes, his chief regret being that he had told his Oregon wife his real name, which led to his capture."

Soper's trial for the murder of Delia and her children was originally scheduled for July but was postponed until the fall of 1897. When the defendant was arraigned in early October, he pled not guilty, and his trial was set for late November. On the first day of the proceedings, November 29, "the largest crowd that ever attended court" in Harrisonville was on hand. Soper's attorneys said their client freely admitted his guilt but that he was of unsound mind when he committed the murders, and they planned to pursue an insanity defense. Soper himself seemed to be in good health and good spirits, and he said he thought he would be acquitted.

During the trial, Soper fully confessed to the killing of his first family, explaining that he was a born murderer who had no control over his actions. Recounting his actions on the night of the murders, Tuesday, April 21, 1891, Soper said he sat up reading after the rest of his family retired. Around 11:00 p.m., when Delia and the kids were sleeping peacefully, he procured an ax, sneaked up to his wife's bed, and dealt her two or three blows to the head. Gillis, the little boy, was sleeping beside his mother, and Soper split the child's head open as well. He then stalked into the room next door and killed his daughter, Maude, with two blows of the ax.

He then washed his hands in a pan of water, which he left sitting on the stove in the kitchen. Afterward, he sat down and calmly wrote out the notes that were found almost three days later. The letter to the *Times* was filled with self-pitying drivel in which he blamed all his trouble on the unfair treatment he had received since his release from the Missouri State Penitentiary, and he said he felt he was being merciful by killing his family, because he didn't want them to suffer as he had.

When Soper had finished writing the notes, he picked up a Bible and read from the Good Book until almost dawn. He then went to the local railroad station and bought a ticket for Kansas City. But instead of going to Clay County to kill the "devil" as he promised in one of his notes, he fled to the state of Washington and then to Oregon, where he was eventually found six years later.

On December 4, 1897, the jury in Soper's case, after deliberating sixteen hours, came back with a verdict of guilty of murder in the first degree. Soper wept when he heard the verdict, as did his mother, who had testified on his behalf during the trial, trying to make a case for insanity.

Ten days after the guilty verdict was rendered, Judge W. W. Wood sentenced Soper to hang on February 4, 1898. His lawyers, however, appealed the verdict to the Missouri Supreme Court, and the execution was postponed pending the outcome of appeal.

In early June of 1898, the *Cass County Democrat* reported that Soper was still "biding his time in the county bastille." He was "very much isolated from the world" with few visitors and only one person who wrote to him—his mother. The rest of his family had abandoned him, but the prisoner was still eating and sleeping relatively well.

Soper continued biding his time in the Harrisonville pokey until early 1899. On February 21 the Supreme Court confirmed the death penalty in his case and reset the execution for March 30, 1899.

HANGING OF SOPER

He Was Executed at Harrison-ville This Morning.

DEAD IN 12 MINUTES.

Slept Well, Ate a Hearty Breakfast and Was Ready When the Sheriff Called Him.

Soper hanging headline from the *Sedalia Democrat*.

In early March, when some of Soper's friends started circulating a petition they planned to present to the governor asking that Soper's death sentence be commuted to life imprisonment, the citizens of Archie organized to oppose the petition, and the governor declined to intervene in the case.

Sometime before Soper's execution date, he finally confessed that he had, indeed, killed his father nineteen years earlier. In his confession, he said he developed a grudge against the old man when he was just six or seven years old and that his hatred grew over the years. Finally making up his mind to kill his father, he started to a literary meeting one evening, doubled back to the Soper farm to ambush his father, and then hurried to the meeting as if nothing was wrong.

On March 28, Soper wrote a letter from his jail cell that was addressed "To the public." Much of it echoed the sniveling tone of his earlier confession. Still seeking to place the blame for his atrocities anywhere but on himself, he said his evilness stemmed from the fact that his mother was living in sin at the time of his conception and throughout the period of gestation so that he was stained with sin at birth. He portrayed himself as an unfortunate, tortured soul, and he felt that right-minded people should understand his anguish and that those who had worked against him had erred.

The next day, which was the day before his scheduled execution, Soper was allowed to go up on the scaffold and test the trap. "I can hardly wait for the time of the execution to come," the condemned man told the sheriff. "The suspense and waiting are worse than the execution can possibly be."

Soper awoke early on March 30 after sleeping only a couple of hours. He ate a sparing breakfast at 4:30 a.m. and then was led to the scaffold by Sheriff F. M. Wooldridge at 5:23 a.m. The sheriff tied Soper's hands and feet and then asked whether he had any last words. When the condemned man declined to speak, Wooldridge adjusted the black cap on his head, bade him farewell and Godspeed, and then pulled the lever that dropped the trap at 5:27 a.m. Soper's neck was broken by the fall, and he was pronounced dead after ten minutes. The body was cut down and placed in a coffin, and a couple of hours later the remains were sent on a train to Clay County for burial.

14

Bald Knobberism Revived

The Lynching of Wife Killer John Wesley Bright

After forty-two-year-old John Wesley Bright killed his wife in Taney County, Missouri, on March 6, 1892, and fled into the woods surrounding his home, a report reached nearby Ozark that, if the killer was caught, "Judge Lynch" was likely to "officiate." After the uxorcide was captured and taken to the Taney County Jail in Forsyth, the rumblings of an extralegal hanging continued, and when it was announced on Saturday the 12th that Bright's preliminary hearing would be carried over into the next week, suspicion mounted that "Judge Lynch would likely terminate the case before Monday morning."

Surprisingly, there were those who passed off the rumors of mob action as mere bluster, but anyone familiar with the record of violence and vigilante justice that had already been carved in the annals of Taney County should not have doubted the gathering mob's determination to carry out its threats. By at least one accounting, the murder of Mrs. Bright brought to seventy the number of people who had been killed in Taney County since the Civil War. The lynching of her husband and the killing of a deputy sheriff in the process would soon add to the total.

On Sunday morning, March 6, John Bright's wife, thirty-eight-year-old Matilda, had started from her house on Roark Creek in northwest Taney County to fetch a pail of water from a nearby spring. Bright, who suspected his wife of being too friendly with a neighbor named Jones and was insanely jealous, followed straightway carrying his gun. The couple's children heard a gunshot, and a few minutes later the father came back alone and told them their mother had been shot by someone at the spring. He warned them not to go near the spring as they might get hurt. Bright then filled his pockets with eggs and other food items and left the house with his gun in hand.

After waiting at the house for some time with mounting concern, the children ventured to the spring against their father's orders and found their mother dead. They quickly sounded an alarm in the neighborhood and Bright was immediately suspected of the murder, based on the story the children told. A posse of about fifty or sixty men promptly organized and went in pursuit of the murderer.

BULLET THROUGH HER HEART.

Wife of John Wesly Bright, of Taney County, Shot.

The Lifeless Body of the Woman Found at the Spring--The Husband the Supposed Murderer.

Springfield Leader headline tells the story of Matilda Bright's murder.

"At each mountain pass," according to a *Springfield Leader* report a few days later, "the party of hunters received new recruits. Soon the woods were full of armed men on horse back and on foot armed with Winchester rifles, shot guns and revolvers." The posse, now numbering about fifty or sixty men, searched "every ravine and cliff where the fleeing criminal might hide.... No terror stricken fugitive from justice could escape that army of men who pressed so resolutely on the heels of John Wesley Bright."

Bright was run to ground on Monday, hiding in the woods not far from his home. He was taken to Forsyth and lodged in the Taney County Jail located just east of the public square. He was held without bond, and his preliminary hearing was scheduled for Saturday, March 12, before justice of the peace W. R. Cox.

However, when the case was called on Saturday morning, it was moved to the jurisdiction of Swan Township justice W. H. Jones. The change of venue caused a delay, and the hearing did not start until mid-day. Only two witnesses, both of whom gave very damaging testimony against Bright, were heard before approaching darkness prompted Judge Jones to adjourn the case until Monday morning.

All throughout the day on Saturday, according to an initial report published in the *Springfield Daily Democrat*, "an unusual number of drunken men were in the streets" of Forsyth, and hints of lynching were frequently heard. A later report in the same newspaper claimed that Matilda Bright's brother, George Gideon, was in Forsyth all day and was often seen talking to small groups of men on the public square, but the problem with this report is that Matilda did not have a brother named George. So, if the man seen on the square was George Gideon, he was probably Matilda's cousin. If, on the other hand, the man on the square was her brother, he was likely Joshua Burt Gideon, but there's no evidence Burt Gideon was instrumental in stirring up mob violence.

Despite the rumors of mob action, Sheriff John Cook was unconvinced that the men threatening to lynch Bright would make such an attempt. Cook told his deputy, George L. Williams, it would be futile to try to stop the vigilantes if they did carry through with their threats and advised Williams not to put up a stiff resistance. One Taney County citizen recollected years later that Cook even went home on Saturday evening, turning the town over to his deputy, but this is incorrect. The sheriff remained in Forsyth all evening but made little effort to prevent the rumored vigilantism.

Williams, however, proved less willing than his boss

to concede to mob action. As the rumors of vigilantism intensified after nightfall, the deputy said he meant to resist any effort to break Bright out of jail. Identifying prominent Taney County attorneys George Taylor and D. F. McConkey as two of the ringleaders who'd been trying during the day to organize mob action against Bright, Williams vowed that, if the two young lawyers and their cohorts succeeded in lynching the prisoner, it would be over his dead body.

The bold pledge would soon be tested.

About nine or ten o'clock Saturday night, twelve to fourteen horsemen, who, according to the *Springfield Leader*, were "disguised beyond recognition," rode into Forsyth from the north and surrounded the jail. (Some estimates place the number of riders considerably higher.) Watching from a store across the street, Deputy Williams rushed to the scene, but accounts differ as to what happened next.

A report in the *Springfield Daily Democrat* published two days after the event said the deputy stationed himself in front of the mob, declared that he recognized their leader, and ordered them to disperse, firing a shot above their heads to punctuate his demand. The mob immediately fired two shots back at Williams, killing him almost instantly.

Taney County author Douglas Mahnkey, writing many years after the event, said that, as soon as the vigilantes surrounded the jail, two of them dismounted and started taking turns pounding with a sledge hammer on the lock that secured the jail's front door. When Deputy Williams strode directly into the mob and jerked the masks off the two men wielding the hammer, he was promptly shot from two different directions.

Regardless of exactly how Williams died, as soon as he was out of the way, the vigilantes broke into the jail and dragged Bright from his cell. They took him to a cemetery about a half mile north of Forsyth near Swan Creek and hanged him from a big oak tree. Somebody among the gang then fired a shot as a signal for the gang to disperse, and the vigilantes faded into the night.

Initials reports said the identity of the lynch mob was "a mystery." The *Springfield Daily Democrat* said one rumor was that the vigilantes came from nearby Christian County, while another was that most of the men were near neighbors of the Brights, who had come to avenge the killing of Matilda Gideon Bright. Yet another story was that the lynching represented a revival of the Bald Knobbers, a notorious vigilante group that dispensed its own brand of justice in Taney County during the mid-1880s, including the lynching of two brothers charged with felonious assault. According to this theory, John Wesley Bright was especially targeted because he had been an anti-knobber during the reign of the Law and Order League, as the Bald Knobbers officially called themselves.

On Monday, May 14, a coroner's inquest, called by Judge Jones, was held over the bodies of Williams and Bright. According to the *Daily Democrat*, the jury "developed no explanation of the affair besides the customary 'by parties unknown.'" After the hearing, both bodies were taken for burial.

When word of the Bright lynching reached Missouri governor David R. Francis, he ordered Sheriff Cook to gather a posse sufficient to hunt down and arrest the vigilantes. He added that, if the sheriff was unable to do so, he would send a state force to help deal with the situation, and he offered a $300 reward for the arrest and conviction of the members of the lynch party.

Cook swore in two new deputies and assigned them the task of identifying the gang that killed Williams and Bright. Based on their investigation, a special grand jury convened about six weeks later, on April 25, and indicted fourteen men for first-degree murder.

As it turned out, there was some truth to the idea that the Bright lynching represented a revival of Bald Knobberism, because several of the men charged with belonging to the recent vigilante mob were prominent Taney County citizens, just as the case had been with the Bald

Knobbers. These included Taylor and McConkey, the two lawyers Williams had suspected as organizers of the mob; county coroner Madison Day; ex-county assessor Bill Stockstill; and Justice of the Peace A. L. "Link" Weatherman. In addition, Day, a former Union captain, had been a member of the original Law and Order League. Other men among the fourteen indicted included Isaac "Big Ike" Lewis and Link Weatherman's brother Samuel.

On May 9, George Friend was arrested in Springfield as another alleged member of the gang that had killed Williams and lynched Bright. In order to get his own charges thrown out or reduced, Friend agreed to turn state's evidence, He was taken to Kansas City, where he told his story to Governor Francis, and Friend's confession was soon thereafter printed in area newspapers, although his identity was not revealed at first.

According to Friend, the main organizers of the mob were George Taylor and Madison Day. Friend also implicated James Delaney, ex-prosecutor of Taney County and stepson of Nat Kinney (the original Bald Knobber chieftain), as playing at least a peripheral part in the mob action.

Friend said Day and Taylor were busy throughout the Saturday of Bright's preliminary hearing firing up the crowd that had come to town to witness the legal proceeding, targeting especially saloon-goers and friends and relatives of Matilda Bright. By late afternoon, about twenty-three men had pledged themselves to help hang Matilda's murderous husband.

At that point, Taylor borrowed a horse from Delaney and rode up Swan Creek to try to recruit men from outside town. A place of rendezvous was selected on Swan Creek about a mile north of Forsyth, and the mob began to assemble there about dark. After about fifteen men had gathered, Day, the old Bald Knobber, administered an oath of secrecy and loyalty to the band, similar to the pledge that had been required of the original Knobbers. After the ceremony, the vigilantes started toward town, on horseback and on foot and gathering additional members along the way.

One man, realizing the gravity of what the band was about to undertake, grew frightened and fled into the woods. Taylor and a few of the other vigilantes wanted to track the deserter down and kill him, but some protested this action. Nine of the vigilantes, whom Friend identified as the ringleaders, went aside to hold a consultation about the matter. These included Day, Taylor, Big Ike Lewis, Bill Stockstill, two of Stockstill's brothers, and three Weatherman brothers.

After the huddle broke up, there was no further mention of the runaway, but someone asked about the fate of Deputy Williams if he resisted the vigilantes as he'd sworn to do. Taylor replied that Sheriff Cook wouldn't put up much fight and that, if Williams tried to interfere, he'd be taken care of. Taylor and Bill Stockstill switched hats, and Stockstill, who'd been made captain of the mob, tied a handkerchief over his face, being the only man who was disguised, according to Friend. The jaunt to Forsyth then resumed.

At the Swan Creek Ford about a quarter of a mile north of town, someone gave a yell, and the grim riders broke into a gallop. The mob had about eight or ten confederates who had stayed in town to monitor the situation there, and one of them, McConkey, had placed a sledgehammer near the jail door before the main body of vigilantes arrived. Taylor, Bill Stockstill, and Friend were at the front of the mob when Deputy Williams hurried to the scene. Williams reached out and raised Taylor's hat, saying, "George Taylor, I have you spotted." Bill Stockstill immediately shot the deputy through the body and then shot him again as Williams turned to face his assassin.

Taylor then picked up the sledge and started battering down the door. Tiring from the task, he handed the hammer to Stockstill, who gave the lock a few licks before handing the sledge to Ike Lewis to complete the work. Taylor then went into the jail and tied a rope around Bright's neck, even as the sheriff and other bystanders hurried to the scene to attend to the fallen deputy.

Stockstill helped Taylor drag Bright out of the jailhouse and put him on a horse behind George Friend. The prisoner was taken to the preselected oak tree at the cemetery north of town, where Stockstill pulled him from the horse and asked him if he had any final words to say. Bright declined to confess to his crime or otherwise comment, and he was promptly swung up on a large limb of the tree.

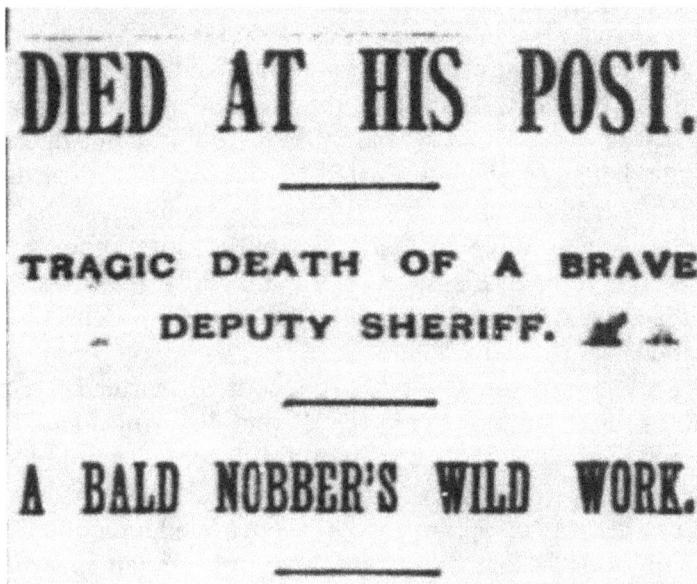

DIED AT HIS POST.

TRAGIC DEATH OF A BRAVE DEPUTY SHERIFF.

A BALD NOBBER'S WILD WORK.

Sedalia Bazoo proclaims the murder of Deputy Williams and the lynching of Bright as the "wild work" of the Bald Knobbers.

After the mob dispersed, Stockstill went back into town and joined the crowd who'd gathered around Deputy Williams's dead body. Stockstill, according to Friend, kept a vigil that night, along with others, over the lawman he had just killed.

Friend was released after telling his story and striking a tentative deal to testify against the other gang members, but he was re-arrested in Springfield on May 17. He and several other suspects, including McConkey, were transported from Springfield back to Forsyth a day or two later.

In all, more than twenty suspects were indicted for the murders of Williams and Bright, although at least three of them were never apprehended. The remaining defendants were arraigned on May 21. The preliminary hearings for fifteen of them began on June 6 with Friend as the star witness. After the state rested its case on June 11, charges against several of the suspects were dismissed for lack of evidence. Twelve were bound over for indictment by a grand jury. These included Taylor, McConkey, Day, Ike Lewis, Bill Stockstill, and the three Weatherman brothers.

On July 20, the grand jury handed down fourteen indictments for the murder of Williams and sixteen for the murder of Bright, with trial in circuit court set for the next day. From the outset, the likelihood of gaining convictions looked slim, because a number of potential witnesses had fled the territory and a majority of the prospective jurors were ex-Bald Knobbers or in sympathy with them. Then, after charges against Friend were officially dropped in exchange for his expected testimony, he suddenly refused to take the stand. Facing a no-win situation, the prosecution dropped all charges.

Nobody ever paid for the either the murder of Deputy Williams or the lynching of John Wesley Bright.

15

A Prussian General Dies on the Gallows

The Hanging of Arthur Duestrow

Twenty-five-year-old Arthur Duestrow was a young man of leisure living off his inheritance when he killed his wife in St. Louis on Valentine's Day Eve of 1894. Son of a wealthy St. Louis businessman, Arthur had always had everything his own way, but this time even the best lawyers money could buy wouldn't save him from the gallows.

Arthur had wed twenty-five-year-old Albertina Leisse four years earlier when he was just twenty-one, and married life seemed to have an ameliorating effect on him at first. Wild and rebellious since his early youth, Arthur was a reckless young man with a reputation as a heavy drinker and a tobacco fiend, but he seemed to settle down after the marriage.

Arthur and Tina moved into a stately home at the edge of the exclusive Compton Heights district, and the couple appeared happy for a while. Arthur lavished gifts on his wife and treated her well.

After a couple of years, though, about the time their son, Louis, was born, young Duestrow resorted to his old ways. He enrolled in the Missouri Medical College "more for the honor of it than anything else," according to the *St. Louis Post Dispatch*, and he appended the title "Doctor" to his name, even though he failed to graduate and never practiced medicine. Instead, he spent his time frequenting saloons and carousing with women of questionable virtue, and he carried a gun everywhere he went.

Meanwhile, his demeanor toward his wife turned nasty. He started cursing and abusing Tina and even fired an

Duestrow as a Medical Student.

Arthur Duestrow as a medical student. From the *St. Louis Post-Dispatch*.

errant shot at her when Louis was about a year old. His erratic behavior caused at least one young woman to quit her job as a servant in the Duestrow household, while another maid allowed that Dr. Duestrow was all right when he was sober but that he was seldom sober. "He used to come home drunk and rave all night," the girl recalled.

Not long after little Louis was born, Arthur took Clara Howard, a young woman who kept an "immoral resort" near downtown St. Louis, as his mistress and started spending much of his time with her. He visited Clara on the snowy morning of February 13, 1894, and left shortly before noon. Wending his way home, he hit several saloons along the three-mile route, and stopped at a livery to hire a driver with a horse and sleigh.

When the sleigh pulled up in front of the Duestrow

residence on Compton Avenue about 4:00 o'clock in the afternoon, Tina saw the carriage from a second floor window and sent her servant girl, Katie Hahn, down to ask whether "the doctor," as she called her husband, was going to take her out sleighing. Katie, with two-year-old Louis in her arms, went downstairs and met a drunken Arthur Duestrow on the front porch just as she opened the door. "You damned bitch," Duestrow swore at the girl as he brushed past her, "you haven't any business to open the door for me."

Duestrow strode up the steps, with Katie trailing behind. Mrs. Duestrow met him at the head of the stairs and asked whether he was going to take her out in the sleigh. "Yes," he snapped, "and get ready in a damn big hurry, too."

Taking Katie with her, Tina went into her room to get ready, while Duestrow took the little boy into his playroom, but Louis soon toddled into his mother's room. Duestrow followed and started berating the two women, calling them "damned bitches" and accusing his wife of keeping a whorehouse.

He tried to hit Katie, but his wife intervened, scolding him for such behavior. "If you hit anybody," she said, "hit me."

Duestrow promptly took his wife up on the invitation, striking her in the face with his hand. He then turned back to Katie in a threatening manner, and Tina again told him to hit her if had to hit someone. The villain struck his wife two more times, the last time causing her to fall toward the bed.

"There, you damned bitches!" Duestrow swore. "I am going."

He picked up the little boy and went madly down the stairs but soon came back with his revolver in his hand. Another angry argument erupted between Tina and her husband over the pistol, and when he started waving it at his wife and Katie, the girl ran out of the room and up to her third-floor quarters.

From her room upstairs, Katie heard the loud quarrelling continue, and she started back down the steps to escape danger. Part way down, she heard a shot and heard Mrs. Duestrow scream that Arthur had shot her. Another shot rang out as she neared the second floor landing, and she paused to glance through an open door into the room from where the shots came in time to see Tina sway on her feet and lurch to the floor. The "doctor" then raised the little boy up, pinioned him against the wall, and placed the revolver against his son's heart. Panic-stricken, Katie turned away, but she heard two more shots ring out in quick succession as she hurried on down the steps.

Katie rushed outside to tell the sleigh driver what had happened. She then fled the scene, and the liveryman drove quickly back to the stable to summon help.

Duestrow made a halfhearted attempt to kill himself, but the bullet barely grazed his head. He then fled on foot into the snowy streets. He hailed a teamster, told him he had killed his wife and child, and asked to be taken to a nearby police substation. Duestrow turned himself in at the station, repeating that he had killed his wife and little boy, and he was arrested.

Investigators hurried to the Duestrow home and found the little boy dead with two gunshot wounds. Tina Duestrow had been shot three times and was in critical condition but still alive. Duestrow's empty revolver was found at the scene.

Interrogated at the substation, Duestrow claimed the shooting was all an accident. He said that, when he arrived home and entered the house, he started to toss his revolver up to his wife on the second floor but she yelled for him not to, because it might go off. He went up the steps, where Tina met him and reached for the weapon. As he handed it to her, it accidentally discharged and kept going off on its own.

Unconvinced by his fantastic story, the police placed him in handcuffs and took him to the Four Courts city jail. Duestrow resented being treated like a common criminal, and he ranted and raved that he couldn't have killed his wife and baby. He spent the night in his cell alternately sobbing and laughing hysterically.

A coroner's inquest on the 14th determined that Louis Duestrow had come to his death at the hands of his father, Arthur Duestrow, and the baby was buried the same day in Bellefontaine Cemetery. Two days later, on February 16, a warrant for murder was issued against the father. His hearing was set for February 20 but was continued until March 20.

Albertina Duestrow died on February 17. An inquest was held the next day, followed by burial in the Saints Peter and Paul Catholic Cemetery in St. Louis. At the hearing on March 20, Duestrow was indicted for murdering his wife. He was arraigned a week later, and the case was set for April 9.

Indicating that they would pursue an insanity defense, Duestrow's team of attorneys, led by former Missouri lieutenant governor Charles P. Johnson, got the case continued until May and were then granted a change of venue to nearby Franklin County. Meanwhile, Duestrow was also indicted for murdering his child.

He was scheduled to go on trial at Union, the Franklin County seat, in mid-September, but the wife murder case was continued until January and the child murder case was continued indefinitely by mutual consent.

When the wife murder case came up in January 1895, Duestrow's lawyers formally filed their insanity plea, and a hearing to determine Duestrow's competence to stand trial began. The proceeding was mainly a "battle of experts," with both sides introducing doctors and other professionals to testify as to the defendant's mental state, based on their interviews with him.

Both sides also called ordinary citizens who had known Duestrow throughout his life. The defense paraded a string of witnesses to the stand to testify that their client was dimwitted, nervous, and addicted to alcohol from a young age and that his behavior was often peculiar. One witness, for instance, said that Duestrow, about midnight one night, accosted a police officer outside a saloon and asked him where the Planter's House was, explaining that he had an engagement to meet General Sherman there. The state's witnesses swore, on the other hand, that they had never seen abnormal behavior from Arthur Duestrow other than drunken belligerence. One man who had known him at the medical college, for instance, said that the defendant's only failing as a student was that he was lazy.

Not only was Duestrow's behavior strange before and at the time of the murders, his lawyers said, but it had been absolutely bizarre since his incarceration. The attorneys produced jail guards and other witnesses who testified that Duestrow made wild claims, saying that his wife and child were still alive, that he had telepathic powers, and that he was the surgeon general of the United States and also a cardinal of the Roman Catholic Church.

Accusing Duestrow of trying to feign insanity, the state produced its own witnesses, including jail guards, who swore they'd never heard the prisoner make any such wild claims or seen him exhibit bizarre behavior. The prosecution also pointed out that how the defendant behaved months after the murders had limited relevance to the question of his sanity at the time of the crime.

Finally, the defense tried to show that Duestrow's parents were both heavy drinkers and, in particular, that his mother had consumed large quantities of alcohol while she was pregnant. The state countered with witnesses who said that neither the father nor the mother were ever more than very moderate drinkers.

The sanity hearing ended in a hung jury, prompting an outburst of criticism from the public and the press over the legal maneuverings of Duestrow's lawyers. The *St. Louis Globe-Democrat*, for instance, railed that the people had seen how

> the lavish use of money could be used to befog the minds of ignorant jurymen with the testimony of medical experts, so called.... This cold-blooded villain stands before the community as a man who is still untried for a heinous crime of which everybody acquainted with the facts knows him to be guilty.

A second sanity hearing began on April 30, and it ended on May 11 with the defendant being declared sane and competent to stand trial for the murder of his wife. However, the trial in late July and early August ended, like the first sanity hearing, in a hung jury.

A new trial was set for January of 1896. It began on the 13th, and the jury came back on the early morning of February 2, after deliberating throughout the night, with a verdict of guilty of murder in the first degree. When the verdict was read, the *Post-Dispatch* said, Duestrow was "the coolest man in the room as far as external appearances," calmly blowing a puff of smoke from his cigarette into the air.

In mid-March, Judge Rudolph Hirzel pronounced a sentence of death by hanging, and the prisoner was taken back to St. Louis for safekeeping. The execution was set for April 22, but it was postponed when Duestrow's lawyers appealed the case to the Missouri Supreme Court.

The case came up for consideration before the high court in January of 1897. One of the defense's main points in its bill of exceptions was that the jury should have been given instructions for a verdict of murder in the second degree, but Justice Thomas Sherwood, reflecting the unanimous opinion of the high court, rejected this argument. "It is well settled in common law...," he wrote, "that, when a homicide is committed in circumstances of great barbarity and cruelty, such brutal malignity will supply the place of malice, and make the act of killing equivalent to a deliberate act of slaughter." The judgment of the lower court was affirmed on January 19, and the new execution date set for February 16, 1897.

About the first of February, a group of St. Louis ladies petitioned Missouri governor Lon Stephens to commute Duestrow's sentence to life imprisonment, but Stephens announced on Monday morning, February 15, the day before the scheduled execution, that he would not interfere in the case. The same morning, even before the governor's announcement, Duestrow, who was now claiming to be Prussian general Count Brandenburg, was taken from St. Louis to Union in preparation for the hanging.

MARCH TO THE GALLOWS.

Duestrow's march to the gallows. From the *St. Louis Post-Dispatch*.

The scaffold was still being built when Duestrow arrived in Union early Monday afternoon, and he could hear the pounding outside his cell after he was placed in the Franklin County Jail. He slept fitfully that night and awoke about 3:00 a.m. on the morning of the 16th. With the coming of dawn, he glanced through the window of his cell at the scaffold and broke into tears. He admitted killing his wife and child but said it wasn't his fault, because something in him made him do it. He said he knew he had to die, but not on a scaffold, because he had invented it and it wasn't legal to kill a man with an apparatus of his own making.

Duestrow was led to the gallows shortly before one p.m. Having resumed the stoic persona of Count Brandenburg, he walked without hesitation and placed himself on the trap. A large crowd pressed in around the stockade, but only a small number of reporters and official observers were allowed inside. The sheriff tied Duestrow's arms and legs and, addressing him by name, asked him whether he had any final words to say.

"I am not Duestrow," the prisoner replied. He then bid farewell to Lieutenant-Governor Johnson and to Countess von Brandenburg.

The sheriff placed the black cap over Duestrow's head and signaled his deputy to cut the rope. The trap fell at exactly one o'clock, and Duestrow was pronounced dead twenty minutes later. Still convinced of his client's insanity, Johnson wanted the body given to science so that Duestrow's brain could be studied. Instead it was placed in a coffin to be turned over to the dead man's sister, Hulda Duestrow, for burial in St. Louis. Hulda had estranged herself from Arthur after his crime and he had denied even knowing anybody named Hulda Duestrow, but she had her brother's body buried in Bellefontaine Cemetery near the son he had killed.

16

They'll Make Me Die Hard

The Lynching of Emmet Divers

After seventeen-year-old newlywed Jennie Cain was found dead near Fulton, Missouri, in July of 1895, twenty-one-year-old Emmet Divers was almost immediately taken into custody as a suspect in the crime. Evidence that Divers had killed the young woman was overwhelming, and he confessed to the murder in short order but denied raping her. After he was lynched a couple of weeks later, though, area newspapers, in defending the vigilantes, seemed set on convincing the public that Jennie had been outraged before she was killed, as though sexual assault on a white woman by a black man was greater justification for mob action than murder. In the eyes of many nineteenth century Americans, it was.

Jennie Cain, who'd been married to twenty-four-year-old farmer John W. Cain a little over two months, spent Monday night, July 22, at a neighbor's house because her husband was working away from home. The next morning after breakfast, Jennie returned to her own house about five miles west of Fulton. When Cain came home later the same morning, he found his bride lying dead in a corner of the room, having been horribly murdered. One end of a rope fastened her arms together, and the other end was tied around her neck. She was naked from the waist down, and her throat was slashed in several places, both the jugular vein and wind pipe severed. Her head lay in a pool of her own blood, and the bed, located at the right of the entrance, had splotches of blood on the cover. "The condition of the bed," said the *Fulton Telegraph*, "indicated that the struggle for her virtue had taken place there.... From indications it appears that the fiend accomplished his devilish purpose on the bed, and afterwards committed the murder." The *Telegraph* also reported that a medical exam confirmed that a sexual assault had taken place.

Cain immediately notified his neighbors of the tragedy, and one of them raced to Fulton to fetch the Callaway County sheriff and coroner. Shortly before noon, Sheriff W. H. Windsor and his deputies picked up the trail of the suspected perpetrator and tracked him across muddy fields to a home two miles south of the crime scene, where they found Emmet Divers covered with blood and placed him under arrest.

The lawmen took Divers back to the Cain home, and the suspect, although protesting his innocence, seemed to know just where they were taking him and "made every turn right up to the place correctly," according to the *Telegraph*. Along the way, the officers searched Divers and found a bloody knife in his possession, and when they got to the Cain place, they found a piece of a suspender buckle beneath the dead woman's body that matched a broken suspender buckle Divers had on. In addition, according to the *Mexico Weekly Ledger*'s inventory of evidence, a piece of cloth that matched the suspect's shirt was found clenched in Jennie's hand, and a lock of her hair was found on Divers's clothes.

Afraid to linger at the Cain farm for fear of a mob forming, Sheriff Windsor took Divers straight to Fulton and lodged him in jail about 1:30 on Tuesday afternoon. That evening, as word of the atrocity reached Fulton and whisperings of mob action spread through the town, the sheriff whisked the prisoner away to Mexico, twenty-five miles to the north. Arriving in the wee hours of Wednesday morning, July 24, Windsor turned the prisoner over to Audrain County sheriff J. W. Stephens, who promptly took Divers on a train to Hannibal, where he spent the night in the city jail. Early Thursday morning, the prisoner was moved to Bowling Green and briefly lodged in the Pike County Jail.

Sheriff Windsor came to Bowling Green later that morning and again took charge of the prisoner. Continuing to play hide and seek with the Callaway County mob, Windsor escorted the suspect to New London and placed him in the Ralls County Jail about 10:00 p.m. Thursday night. Not satisfied that New London was far enough away from Fulton to prevent mob violence, Sheriff Windsor again moved Divers late Friday night, this time to St. Louis, where the lawman and his prisoner arrived at 4:00 o'clock on the morning of Saturday, July 27.

Windsor had Divers placed in the Four Courts jail with plans to move him back to Callaway County for a preliminary hearing in about three weeks. "The excitement," the sheriff predicted, "will probably have somewhat subsided by that time."

He couldn't have been more wrong.

Interviewed in St. Louis, Windsor was convinced of the prisoner's guilt. He said Divers had previously been charged with sexual offenses—an assault on his wife's nine-year-old sister and "trouble of a similar character about a negro woman." In addition, the sheriff said Divers "comes of a bad family. Two of his brothers have been convicted as assaulting women and one of them is still in the penitentiary." (Prison records confirm the latter assertion.)

A day or two after his arrival in St. Louis, Divers admitted that he had killed Jennie Cain. He said he left home about 9:00 a.m. on the day of the crime and reached the Cain residence about an hour later. He walked in through the open door and found the young woman sitting by the bed cutting out quilt pieces. He asked if anybody else was at home, and she said no. He told her to give him the ring she had on her finger, and when she refused and started resisting his efforts to take it from her, he knocked her to the floor with his fist. When she started to rise, he tied her up, but she still kept trying to fight him. So he cut her throat. After "persistent questioning," he also reportedly confessed to sexually assaulting his victim. Divers then expressed a desire to be hanged at the jail in St. Louis rather than be taken back to Callaway County.

Callaway County remained in a "white heat" throughout late July and early August over the assault and murder of Jennie Cain, and as the time for Divers's preliminary hearing approached, as many as five or six hundred vigilantes in and around Fulton organized to take the law into their own hands as soon as the prisoner was brought back. They made a not-so-secret pact that Divers would be burned alive—taken back to the cabin where he committed his crime, tied inside, and the torch applied.

Despite the obvious determination of the would-be lynchers, local authorities did very little to forestall the expected mob violence, other than issue a decree that all saloons in Fulton be shut down. A rumor developed that the state militia might be brought in to protect the prisoner, but no such action was taken. And when word leaked on August 14 that two special deputies had departed from eastern Callaway County for St. Louis to bring Divers back, a huge mob began patrolling the streets in and around Fulton in squads, guarding every entrance to the county seat.

The two deputies, Ed Buckner and John Buchanan, arrived in St. Louis on Wednesday afternoon the 14th. As they were getting ready to leave with their prisoner, Divers repeated his wish that he could be hanged in St. Louis. Bidding his fellow inmates goodbye, he said,

> "You'll never see me alive agin, for sure. When I get to Fulton I will be strung up. I killed that woman, but didn't intend to. It's a lie that I ravished her, but it's no use talking, for when they get me up there at Fulton, I will be a dead nigger.... They will make me die hard."

The deputies and their prisoner left St. Louis about 4:00 p.m. on the 14th, taking a train to New Florence, about thirty-five miles east of Fulton. Late that night, they secured a conveyance and started overland for Fulton. A couple of miles west of Calwood, a small community about twelve miles northeast of Fulton, the carriage was suddenly surrounded by a mob of about twenty-four masked men. Punctuating their demand with "a display of shooting irons," according to the *Auxvasse Review*, the vigilantes ordered the lawmen to turn around and go back toward Calwood. When Buckner and Buchanan pled with the mob to let the law take its course, the vigilantes retorted that they didn't want to hurt the lawmen but that they meant business and were going to take the prisoner one way or another. Realizing the grim determination of the mob, the deputies offered no further resistance.

The procession backtracked to Calwood and stopped on a bridge crossing Auxvasse Creek about one o'clock Thursday morning, August 15. After Divers was dragged out of the wagon, one end of a rope was tied around a brace on the bridge and the other end around his neck. He was then either forced to jump or, more likely, shoved off the bridge. Ten minutes later, according to the *Review*, "his worthless body was dangling between heaven and earth."

When word of the lynching reached Fulton in the wee hours of the morning, the mob that had been patrolling the streets around the town, consisting of several hundred men, galloped to Calwood at full speed. When they saw the corpse swinging from the bridge, they rent the night air with angry curses that they'd been denied the pleasure of burning a man alive. They accused the sheriff and other legal authorities of conspiring to prevent a terrible scene in Fulton by tipping off the relatively small crowd who'd hanged Divers as to the prisoner's whereabouts and by giving their unofficial blessing to the lynching.

Sometime after daylight on Thursday morning, the county coroner impaneled a jury and visited the scene of the lynching. The jury reached the usual verdict that the victim had come to his death at the hands of persons unknown.

A mob of at least two hundred men then took possession of the body and brought it to Fulton in a wagon about noon or shortly after. They flung off the cover that concealed

DIVERS IS DEAD.

The Negro Fiend Swung From The Calwood Bridge.

OFFICERS AND PRISONER LEFT THE TRAIN AT NEW FLOR-ENCE AND WERE DRIV-ING ACROSS THE COUNTRY.

Hanged at 1 O'Clock Thursday Morning, Nine Miles East of Fulton—The Mob Met With No Resist-ance From the Two Deputies.

The *Mexico Weekly Ledger* tells the tale of Emmett Divers's fate.

Divers's body, and "fully a thousand people took turns in viewing the distorted features of the corpse," said the *Fulton Telegraph*. Forming a procession, the mob marched with the corpse around the courthouse, shouting "Let the law take its course" in mockery of what they thought was collusion between law officers and the lynch party. The angry mob then took the body to the fairgrounds west of town, where it was suspended from the limb of a tree and filled with bullets.

Thirty minutes later, the corpse was brought back to the square and suspended from the cross beam of a telephone pole in front of the courthouse.

The body was left hanging until mid-afternoon, and hundreds of the morbidly curious witnessed the ghastly sight. About 3:15 p.m. the corpse was cut down and taken to a potter's field just outside Fulton and interred. City authorities would not allow burial within the city limits. As Divers was laid to rest, still pinned to his ragged clothes was the following note:

> We, the jury, find that Emmet Divers was hung by law, run away from Fulton by law, protected by law, and a few men selected by the officers of Fulton to hang him by law.
>
> Coroner's Jury.

The lynching of Emmet Divers came under criticism from the St. Louis press, but the local newspapers strongly defended the mob action. Responding to a *Globe-Democrat* editorial calling for funds to be raised to aid in the prosecution of the men who lynched Divers, the *Mexico Weekly Herald*, for example, responded,

> "Not a cent for the prosecution, but millions for defense in a case of this kind. No arm but that of a sentimental idiot would have been stretched forth to save the life of Emmet Divers, the negro who was swung to a railroad bridge…on Thursday morning for the rape and murder of a white woman."

17
A Record for Speedy Justice

The Sawyer Murders and the Hanging of Ed Perry

On Saturday afternoon, May 23, 1896, some pedestrians were passing the Sawyer residence along present-day Hunter Road about a mile east of Ava, Missouri, when they noticed an unusual number of flies swarming around the house's windows. Stepping closer to the dwelling, which sat thirty feet off the roadway, they smelled a terrible odor emanating from the home. Rather than attempt to enter the residence, they continued on to Ava to report their findings, and two constables and a deputy sheriff went out to the Sawyer home to investigate. Going inside, the men were almost overcome by the smell of decaying human flesh, and they discovered the bodies of Lafayette Sawyer; his wife, Sarah; and their grown son, Earnest E., stuffed under a bed and covered with bed clothing and a carpet.

Earnest Sawyer had been stabbed several times and had a broken jaw. Blood evidence and manure on his clothes suggested that he had been killed in the barn after putting up a terrific struggle. It was thought the murderer had then gone to the house and killed the father with a blow to the head with a blunt instrument. "A second blow," said the *Kansas City Daily Journal*, "scattered the brains of Mrs. Sawyer over the bed." Earnest Sawyer's body was dragged to the house, and all three were placed under the bed. A note was found on the front window of the house saying that the family had gone to Ozark and would be back the following Monday or Tuesday. It was signed "E. E. Sawyer," but the theory was that the killer had probably written the note to try to allay the suspicions of anybody who might come to the door. Based on when the Sawyers had last been seen, it was thought the murders had probably taken place the previous Wednesday evening. The only motive anyone could come up with for the crime was robbery, although the Sawyers were not thought to have much money or other possessions. In reporting the story, newspapermen compared the crime in heinousness to the notorious murder of the Meeks family that had occurred in northern Missouri about two years earlier.

The Sawyer family, from the *Springfield Republican*.

A young man named Edward W. Perry was immediately suspected of killing the Sawyers, because he had been seen in Ava on Wednesday in company with Earnest Sawyer and had since disappeared. "A worthless fellow," according to newspaper reports, the twenty-one-year-old Perry was originally from Belleville, Kansas, but he had an aunt who lived northeast of Ava and he had been "loafing about" the town for several months.

Ed Perry, from the *Springfield Republican*.

On Sunday, May 24, the day after the bodies were found, Perry was arrested at his aunt's home north of Ava.

Because Douglas County was temporarily without a sheriff, Prosecuting Attorney E. H. Farnsworth made the arrest. Since Douglas County also lacked a jail, Farnsworth took Perry at first to Mansfield and turned him over to a deputy with the idea of sending him by train to West Plains for incarceration in the Howell County Jail. However, Farnsworth changed his mind, and Perry was instead taken back to Ava in a horse-drawn vehicle.

On the trip back, Perry made a confession upon a promise of protection from potential mob violence. His story was that a man connected to the Forepaugh and Sells Brothers Circus whom he had met on a train between Springfield and Mansfield a month and a half earlier and who held a grudge against the Sawyers had promised him and two other young men $200 apiece to commit the crime. Perry said he and his two sidekicks, Arthur Douglas and Jack Baker, had sneaked up on the Sawyer cabin near dawn on Wednesday morning, May 20, to lay in wait but that he fell asleep on the ground and awoke to the sounds of a struggle going on in the Sawyer barn. Douglas and Baker had called Earnest Sawyer from the house, and the old man and woman had followed their son to the barn. Perry said he entered the building in time to help finish off Earnest Sawyer but played no part in the deaths of the parents, although he confessed to helping drag all three bodies back into the house. After the murders, the three men rifled through the house and found $156 in cash, which they divided.

They also rounded up a lot of clothes, trinkets, and anything else of value they could lay their hands on and, after hiding out most of the day, loaded the loot into the Sawyer wagon, hitched the Sawyers' horses to it, and started toward Springfield on Wednesday night. A short distance from Ava, Baker left the other two men, but Perry and Douglas continued on to Springfield, where they sold the wagon and team. Perry returned by train on Saturday night to Mansfield, where he lay over at the Arlington Hotel, and then came on the next day to his aunt's house, where he was arrested shortly after his arrival. Perry claimed that he had again crossed paths with the anonymous circus man on his return train trip from Springfield to Mansfield but had received only an assurance that the man would send Perry a postcard in care of the Mansfield post office arranging a time and place that the promised blood money would be paid.

Few people believed Perry's fantastic yarn. Not only did the story seem incredible on its face, but certain other evidence suggested it was not true. For instance, Perry had bruises on his wrist, indicating that he had been involved in a desperate fight instead of coming into the deadly fray with the Sawyers after all three victims were incapacitated, as he claimed.

Anticipating that a mob might try to take the law into its own hands just as Perry had feared, authorities locked the prisoner in a room of the Douglas County courthouse under a strong guard upon reaching Ava on Sunday evening. Outraged citizens had been shrilling for vengeance ever since the horrific crime had been discovered and Ed Perry's likely participation in it ascertained, and Perry's implausible tale did little to satisfy their thirst for retribution. Angry groups of citizens clustered together throughout Sunday night and into the next day talking of vigilante justice, while Farnsworth and other distinguished citizens tried to appease the rabble-rousers with assurances that the perpetrator of the crime would be quickly and severely dealt with in the courts if they would let the law take its course.

When word of Perry's dubious story about the murder of the Sawyers reached Springfield on Sunday, law officers there undertook an investigation into his claims relative to his movements during his brief sojourn in that city. After learning that Arthur Douglas had left Springfield on Tuesday to deliver a load of household goods to Ava for a person who was moving there, officers arrested Douglas at his home in Springfield and briefly detained him on suspicion. However, it was soon determined that he had not departed Springfield until 10:00 a.m., meaning he could not have made it to Ava in time to have participated in the murder of the Sawyer family, which, according to Perry's story, occurred near dawn on Wednesday. Douglas soon convinced authorities that he had not even met Perry until Thursday night when he overtook him at a spring about four miles east of the James River during his return trip from Ava. Perry had introduced himself as Ed Wilson, and the two men had continued the journey together into Springfield and arrived about 11:00 p.m. Thursday night.

After spending the night at Douglas's home, Perry, still calling himself Ed Wilson, tried to sell the Sawyer team and horses in Springfield the next day but had trouble doing so because the first couple of prospective buyers were reluctant to make the purchase without a clear title. Perry tried to convince them by explaining that he had acquired the wagon and team while traveling with the Lemmon Brothers Circus, which he had recently quit, but the men remained unconvinced.

On Saturday, Perry finally found a horse trader named Gilbert who paid him $56 for the wagon and team. After the sale, Perry splurged on a new suit of clothes and went to a barber shop to have his hair trimmed and his mustache shaved off. On Saturday night, while standing near the train depot in company with Arthur Douglas, Perry suddenly bolted away and jumped aboard the eastbound Memphis train after it was already in motion, yelling to Douglas that he was going back to Mansfield.

News that Perry had sold the Sawyer wagon and team in Springfield under an assumed name and had falsely accused Douglas of being an accomplice in the family's murder only reinforced the belief around Ava that Perry's story was a "bogus confession," as one newspaper called it, meant to mitigate his own guilt. When he changed his story two days after his arrest to implicate his aunt's husband, William Yost, many observers remained convinced that he was still lying and was only trying to shift part of the blame for his heinous crime to someone else.

Perry gave a thorough account of his new version of the crime in a letter of confession he wrote on Tuesday, May 26, to his mother in Belleville. He told her that he and William Yost had plotted the crime together, although they'd originally planned only to rob the family. On the morning of the murders, Perry went to the Sawyer home and lured Earnest from the house by telling him he had a sick horse in his barn. When young Sawyer arrived at the stable, Will Yost struck him in the head with a blunt object, and Perry finished him off with a metal pipe. Aroused by the commotion, the father and mother appeared at the barn. Perry hit the old man a blow with the pipe and then turned his attention to the woman, striking her over the head twice, while Yost finished off Mr. Sawyer with several more licks.

Afterward, the killers dragged all three bodies into the house and stuffed them under the bed. Of the $156 Perry and his uncle found in the house, Yost kept all the paper money, $144, while Perry got only $12 in coins, plus whatever he could get out of the wagon, team, and the household items taken from the home. Perry confirmed everything Arthur Douglas had said about the circumstances of their meeting and their movements in Springfield, and he said the reason he went back to his aunt's home on Sunday was that he and Yost had prearranged to rendezvous there on that day.

After Perry's latest story, William Yost was arrested and charged, along with Perry, in the Sawyer case, although many people still doubted Yost's involvement in the crime. Perry's trial began on Monday, June 1 at a special session of the Douglas County Circuit Court with Judge W. N. Evans presiding, and it lasted into the next day. The courtroom was packed on both days, and the largest crowd ever seen on the streets of Ava milled about the town. The case was given to the jury at 2:45 p.m. on June 2, and they returned in twenty minutes with a verdict of guilty of murder in the first degree.

Judge Evans postponed pronouncement of sentence on Perry until after Yost's trial, which was slated to begin the next day. However, when Yost's case came up on

Wednesday, he was granted a change of venue to neighboring Howell County. Evans then sentenced Perry to hang on July 31. The *Taney County Republican* at Forsyth commented, "This breaks the record in the state of Missouri for speedy justice. The discovery of the crime, the arrest, trial and conviction of one of the murderers only consuming ten days' time gives Douglas County the palm."

Perry's case was appealed to the Missouri Supreme Court, and his execution date was postponed pending the outcome of his appeal. The prisoner was transferred to the Greene County Jail in Springfield for safekeeping while awaiting the high court's decision.

In October, Yost's trial began at West Plains, and Perry was taken there to testify. Perry said he had told his initial story about Arthur Douglas to shield his uncle but that he had decided to tell the truth after he heard that Yost was one of the men encouraging mob violence against him. However, Perry reportedly made several contradictory statements in his testimony, which constituted the only evidence against Yost. Public sentiment seemed to be in Yost's favor, and he was acquitted on October 23. Asked about the verdict back in Springfield the next day, Perry said simply that the Howell County jury had "made a mistake."

In late November, the Missouri Supreme Court confirmed the lower court's verdict in the Perry case and set December 30 as the new date for the prisoner's execution. Perry's mother, Jane, accompanied by other family members, came to Missouri from Kansas to plead for mercy for her son. Mrs. Perry said Ed had fallen from a pile of lumber when he was a child and received an injury to his head that permanently damaged his thinking ability. A Springfield lawyer, T. B. Love, volunteered his services pro bono and presented Mrs. Perry's case to Missouri governor William J. Stone. The governor refused to commute Perry's sentence but did grant a reprieve, postponing the execution until January 30, 1897.

Upon learning of Mrs. Perry's efforts on behalf of her

son, a group of indignant citizens from Douglas County petitioned the governor not to entertain any more requests for commutation or to grant any more reprieves. The petitioners felt the people of Douglas County had spoken and that their will should not be interfered with by any "pettifogging lawyer" or overridden by the governor.

On January 5, Douglas County's new sheriff, George Johnson, came to Springfield and escorted Perry to the Howell County Jail at West Plains. The only reason Johnson could offer for the transfer was that Perry had "too many friends in Springfield."

There were, indeed, people in Springfield who viewed Perry's case with more sympathy than most citizens around Ava. The *Springfield Republican* editor, for instance, decried the vengeful mood in Douglas County and blamed, in particular, the *Ava Farm Record* for stirring up anger against Perry both before and after his trial. The *Republican* said that the citizens of Douglas County were not as overwhelmingly in favor of executing Perry as the Ava newspaper claimed and that a significant portion of them favored life imprisonment instead. The *Republican* editor concluded that Perry had not gotten a fair trial because his case had been rushed through the Douglas County Circuit Court to forestall a lynching and his court-appointed attorneys, who were inept to begin with, had not had time to prepare an adequate defense. Also, the Springfield newspaperman did not think it was right that William Yost had been granted a change of venue and Ed Perry had not, even though both men were on trial for the same crime.

In mid-January, Perry's mother petitioned Missouri's new governor, Lon Stephens, for another reprieve, but it was refused. Ed Perry's time was running out.

On January 25, Sheriff Johnson and E. H. Farnsworth (who was no longer county prosecutor) were summoned to West Plains after a rumored plot to break Ed Perry out of the Howell County Jail was uncovered. The prisoner was taken back to Ava and placed once again in the courthouse under heavy guard to await his awful destiny.

Perry slept hardly at all on the night before he was scheduled to die, finally lapsing into a fitful sleep about 5:00 o'clock on the morning of January 30. When he was roused a few hours later, he refused to eat but did accept a glass of wine that was offered him.

By mid-morning, a large crowd estimated at about 4,000 people had gathered on and around the courthouse grounds in Ava in anticipation of Perry's hanging. Ex-Prosecuting Attorney Farnsworth appeared on the courthouse steps about 10:30 to address the crowd, assuring them that the citizens of Douglas County were law-abiding people and that, contrary to what some "metropolitan" newspaper might say, Ed Perry had indeed received a fair trial.

At 11:00 a.m., Perry asked to see his spiritual advisor, the Rev. J. H. Bridges, and the preacher was summoned. Perry told the minister it was hard to part with life but he was prepared. He said he was guilty of the Sawyer murders but that William Yost was equally guilty and it was not fair that he should die and his uncle go free. He asked Bridges to speak to the crowd on his behalf, and the minister consented. The sheriff and a deputy escorted the two men to a bandstand that sat in the courtyard, from where the Rev. Bridges spoke, repeating basically what Perry had asked him to say. After Bridges finished, Perry stepped forward and said, "People of Douglas County, this is the last time you will ever see me alive. I am not afraid to die. God bless you, is my prayer."

The prisoner was taken back to the courthouse, where his mother was waiting to bid him a final, heartrending goodbye. Mrs. Perry remained with her son until the officers escorted him away on his final promenade about 1:15 in the afternoon.

During the march to the scaffold, a guard walked on either side of the condemned man, but Perry did not have to be assisted. At the scaffold, he mounted the steps with no sign of outward concern.

A stockade about fifteen feet high had been erected

around the scaffold, and only 200 spectators had tickets allowing them inside to view the execution. The rest of the crowd had to content themselves by climbing into trees, finding other high vantage points, or else trying to sneak a peek through cracks in the stockade.

When Sheriff Johnson asked Perry whether he had anything to say, Perry denounced E. H. Farnsworth, saying the former county prosecutor had promised to help try to get Perry's death sentence commuted to life imprisonment in exchange for his testimony against Yost but had instead done everything he could against Perry. The condemned man repeated his claim that he was not the only one guilty. Then he turned to Farnsworth, took the ex-prosecutor's hand, and told him that he forgave him for all he had done against him. He also shook hands with the sheriff and his deputies before stepping onto the trap and saying to Sheriff Johnson, "Now, Sheriff, do your duty."

A black cap was placed over Perry's head and the rope adjusted around his neck. The sheriff pulled the lever, and Perry shot through the trap at 1:37 p.m. He was pronounced dead fifteen minutes later, and his body was cut down and placed in a waiting coffin. According to one contemporaneous report, the execution, which still stands as the only legal hanging in Douglas County history, was "a success in every particular."

Mrs. Perry took charge of her son's body and took it back to Belleville, where a funeral service and burial was held on February 1.

Deliberately Planned and Skillfully Executed

The Lynching of Ras Brown

When twenty-two-year-old Erastus "Ras" Brown left his home near St. Clair, Missouri, on or about Friday, July 2, 1897, he told his young wife, Julia, he would bring back medicine for their sick baby. The next thing Julia heard about her husband was that he was accused of assaulting a young white woman, and rumors of lynching the "black fiend" were running rampant. A teenage mother of two, Julia was worried sick about her deathly ill child, and now her husband of less than two years was in deep trouble.

After leaving St. Clair, Ras tramped toward Gray Summit, almost fifteen miles distant, where he'd grown up. Whether he ever made it to Gray Summit is not certain, but what is known is that he didn't made it back home. Instead, he got sidetracked late on the morning of the 2nd when he saw twenty-one-year-old Annie Foerving walking along the road near Villa Ridge, between St. Clair and Gray Summit.

Annie, a "pretty country girl," had been to Villa Ridge to do some shopping and was on her way home with her basket of purchases on her arm when she left the main road and started down a wooded path about a mile southeast of the village. According to her later story, someone sprang out of the brush and hit her in the head with a rock, knocking her to the ground. Stunned but still conscious, she sat up and saw a black man hovering over her. She screamed and struggled as he pounced on her, but he quickly choked her into insensibility. When she regained consciousness, her attacker was gone.

But that's not the story that spread like wildfire in the

Villa Ridge vicinity and that was initially reported in area newspapers. A "mulatto ravisher" had assaulted Miss Foerving, he had been frightened away by nearby farmhands responding to her frantic cries for help, and whether he had "accomplished his purpose" was uncertain. Even after two doctors examined Annie and found her suffering only from a scalp wound and "nervous prostration," many in the community remained convinced that she had been sexually violated, and reports continued to assert that her condition was critical.

As soon as Annie was rescued, she was taken to the nearby farmhouse of John Sweet and made comfortable. Upon hearing her story, a posse of Sweet's neighbors set out to find the villain who'd attacked her, and other search parties soon joined the hunt.

Ras Brown, or "Black Rastus" as many white folks called him, was immediately suspected of the crime. Originally from the area, he had been seen hanging around the vicinity in recent days, and he seemed to fit Miss Foerving's description of her attacker. One report also claimed he'd been previously suspected of assaulting two young women of his own race. Another report countered that he had "borne a good reputation" until about a year previous but had since "been 'trifling' and suspicioned of petty stealing."

The posse that formed at Sweet's place located Brown on Saturday morning along a railroad track near St. Clair and arrested him without incident. They took him aboard a spring wagon back to Sweet's farmhouse, where Annie was still being tended to, and she reportedly sat up in bed and cried out that he was the man who'd attacked her.

Realizing that mob fever had spread throughout the Villa Ridge area since the attack on Annie Foerving, the men at the Sweet place plotted to prevent a lynching. They sent word to the other posses that they had taken Ras Brown to the woods to "attend to his case," when, in fact, three of their number started with the captive toward the Franklin County seat at Union ten miles away. The threesome arrived Saturday night, and Brown was lodged in the county jail.

THE VICTIM OF THE MOB.

Sketch of Ras Brown, from the *St. Louis Post-Dispatch*.

When the other men who'd been hunting Brown realized they'd been duped, cries for vigilante justice flared anew. Late Sunday night, July 4th, a loosely organized band of about twenty or twenty-five men from the Villa Ridge area rode to Union, arriving on the outskirts in the wee hours of Monday morning. Here they left three men to watch their horses while the rest of the party came into town on foot.

Half of them went directly to the jail, and the other half went to jailer L. H. Gehlert's nearby dwelling. Answering a knock on his door, Gehlert was confronted by eight or ten men who said they had a prisoner to deliver. When the jailer asked for the prisoner's commitment papers, one of the men started to reach into his pocket as if to retrieve the papers but suddenly grabbed Gehlert and demanded the keys to the jail so they could "hang that black SOB." The powerful, 250-pound jailer hurled his assailant over the bannister of his front porch and onto the ground. Before the others could react, Gehlert retreated into his house and slammed the door shut. Retrieving his revolver, he told the mob he would shoot them all if they didn't leave immediately. Despite being armed themselves, the mob, some of whom were masked, promptly "straggled out of town in all kinds of gaits except a slow walk." Thus ended what the *St. Louis Post Dispatch* called "a feeble attempt at lynching the negro ravisher."

But the vigilantes of Villa Ridge would be heard from again.

In the meantime, Brown was brought before a justice of the peace on Tuesday, July 6. Waving a preliminary hearing, he was remanded to jail to await the action of a grand jury. Brown, who'd spent most of his time praying since his incarceration, admitted attacking Miss Foerving but said his only motive was robbery and that he had taken "no undue liberties" with her.

On Tuesday, the same day Ras was taken before the justice of the peace, his wife, Julia, started for Gray Summit with her sick baby to see a doctor, but the infant died in her arms during the trip. The next morning, her father, Governor Baker, trekked to nearby Pacific and reported that Julia was heartsick with grief over her dead child and that she and her mother-in-law were "nearly crazed" with worry over Ras's fate. Rumors that Brown had already been lynched were still afloat, and Baker went to the local newspaper in Pacific to find out whether the rumors were true.

Although her husband's reputation might have been less than sterling, Julia and her family were well liked in the community and had always gotten along with white folks. Her father was poor, but he was considered "respectful, industrious and honest." Ras's parents, Frank and Agnes Brown, were also known as "respectable colored people."

About 1:30 Saturday morning, July 10, another mob, twice as large as the group that had made a halfhearted attempt to lynch Brown five days earlier, rode into Union from the direction of Villa Ridge. Also better organized and more determined than the previous bunch, the heavily armed and partially disguised mob broke into two columns as they neared the jail. One column headed for the jailer's home, while the other rode to a boarding house where the sheriff stayed. They detailed squads to guard against comings and goings at the lawmen's residences and also sent out sentries to watch the streets leading to the jail.

The rest of the vigilantes then descended on the jail. Taking tools from a spring wagon they'd brought along, they battered down the outside door with two or three blows from a sledgehammer. Once inside the building, they quickly knocked down a wooden door that led upstairs, where the cells were located. At the top of the stairs, a large iron door with a heavy bolt lock denied access to the main jail corridor. Using a sledgehammer and chisel, the mob took fifteen minutes to cut through the bolt.

Outside on the street, the ruckus at the jail attracted the curiosity of late-night bystanders and aroused a few citizens from their beds. Anyone who got close to the scene was warned away, and a messenger sent to summon the sheriff was also intercepted. County judges Marshall Coleman and Robert Denny, however, managed to get near enough to the jail for Coleman to remonstrate with the mob, imploring the vigilantes not to take the law into their own hands. His pleas fell on deaf ears, and the judges were warned to get back.

BREAKING IN THE JAIL DOOR.

Sketch of mob breaking into jail to lynch Ras Brown. *St. Louis Post Dispatch.*

After finally breaking through the large iron door, the mob upstairs made quick work of an inside door leading directly to the jail corridor. Ras Brown, who had been singing and praying earlier in the evening, sat in his cell trembling with fright as the mob went to work on his cell door. It yielded quickly to the sledge, and the crowd stormed in and bound the prisoner's arms and legs. Someone put a rope around his neck, and he was carried from his cell and down the steps amid curses and shouts from the mob.

Brown was placed in the spring wagon that had carried the tools, and the mob retreated out of town with their captor along the same route they'd come in on. About a half mile east of Union, they crossed the Bourbeuse River and stopped at a big willow tree about an eighth of a mile beyond the bridge. Part of the mob guarded the bridge to keep curious onlookers from Union away from the scene. The end of the rope opposite the noose around Brown's neck was tossed over a limb overhanging the road. Brown, already lifeless or nearly so, was stood up in the wagon as the rope was made fast. Then the wagon was driven out from under him. After staying just long enough to make sure Brown was dead, the mob retreated to the east, and some of the curious citizens of Union crossed the bridge to gawk at the body as it dangled in the night air.

After gazing at the corpse a while, the onlookers went back to town and informed the sheriff and other citizens what had happened. The sheriff and the coroner went out to the scene, cut the body down, and brought it back to the jail, where the coroner held an inquest about 9:00 a.m. the same morning. The jury concluded that Erastus Brown came to his death by hanging at the hands of parties unknown to the jury.

Local citizens around Union passed off the travesty of justice philosophically, observing that the only thing that surprised them was that the lynching bee hadn't been held as a Fourth of July celebration. And one newspaper praised the vigilante action as "deliberately planned and skillfully executed."

Julia Brown and her in-laws were notified of Ras's fate, and they came to Union to claim the body. Ras was buried near Gray Summit, where he had grown up.

A Franklin County grand jury that met during the September 1897 term investigated the lynching of Ras Brown, but it found "insufficient evidence to return indictments against any of the perpetrators."

And what became of Julia Brown? Having lost her husband and an infant child in the space of five days, she was now a teenage widow with another baby still to take care of, but the circumstances of her life after she came to Union with Frank and Agnes Brown to take charge of her husband's body have not been traced.

19

Kissin' Cousin Turned Killin' Cousin

The Curious Case of Ernest Clevenger

At Ernest Clevenger's murder trial in November of 1899 in the Circuit Court of Clay County, Missouri, defense lawyers James C. Davis and Theodore Emerson argued that their client was insane. Claiming that insanity had run in the Clevenger family for years, the attorneys added that Ernest's parents were first cousins and that all the children from the marriage were "weak minded." The events surrounding Clevenger's crime seem to lend a certain credence to Davis and Emerson's line of argument, but it didn't save their client from the gallows.

Clevenger had come from Tennessee to Missouri in the early 1890s to live with relatives in the Fishing River area of southeast Clay County. Sometime prior to the fall of 1898, he started living with and working for Jerome Clevenger, his father's first cousin. The twenty-three-year-old Ernest took a liking to Jerome's seventeen-year-old daughter, Jennie, and started escorting her to social functions. He soon declared his love for her, but the girl didn't quite share his passion.

Jennie's father didn't like the match either. Jerome Clevenger thought his young kinsman was too disreputable for his daughter, and he might have decided, too, that there'd already been enough intermarriage in the Clevenger clan. When he learned that the relationship between Ernest and Jennie had turned serious, at least in Ernest's mind, he kicked the young man off his farm and told him not to come back.

Young Clevenger, though, wasn't easily deterred. Despite Jerome Clevenger's ultimatum, Ernest kept coming around trying to see Jennie. Then, when he learned that another young man of the neighborhood, George Allen, had started courting her, he became crazed with jealousy. At one point, he told Jennie that if she married Allen, they would "never have no peace." On another occasion, an acquaintance, James McAfee, remarked to Ernest Clevenger that Allen seemed to be having better luck with the girls than they were, and Clevenger replied, yes, but that if Allen wasn't careful, he'd "get shot in two."

On Thursday, December 8, 1898, Clevenger spent the day drinking with another young man, Charles West. About four o'clock in the afternoon, they showed up under the influence at Miltondale, about a mile north of the Clevenger School House. Clevenger, who was said to have a good disposition except when he was drinking, declared that he was looking for George Allen, because he had a score to settle with him.

A few hours later, knowing that Allen had an engagement with Jennie that evening, Clevenger rode double behind West on the latter's horse to the Clevenger School to see whether the couple might be attending the revival meeting in session there. Jennie and her beau weren't there, but, as Clevenger and West were leaving, they met the couple in a buggy a short distance away.

Clevenger tried to flag them down, but Allen whipped up his team and sped away. West put spurs to his horse and rode up beside the buggy. As the buggy slowed, Clevenger tried to pull Allen from the driver's seat, but Allen shook him off and continued to the school house.

Allen and his girlfriend entered and sat near a stove in the middle of the large meeting room next to Jennie's fifteen-year-old sister, Della. Clevenger soon followed and took a seat just behind the group after the divine service had already begun. Once or twice during the meeting, he got up and went outside, and when he came back, he took a seat near the rear of the room.

At the end of the service, the preacher asked everyone to stand for the benediction, and when they did, Clevenger stalked toward Jennie and her group. He pulled out a revolver, and muttering "I'll show you," shot Allen in the back of the head. He collapsed, and Jennie grabbed him, trying to support him, just as Clevenger turned to fire at her. The weight of Allen's body pulled her down, and the shot missed, hitting Della instead.

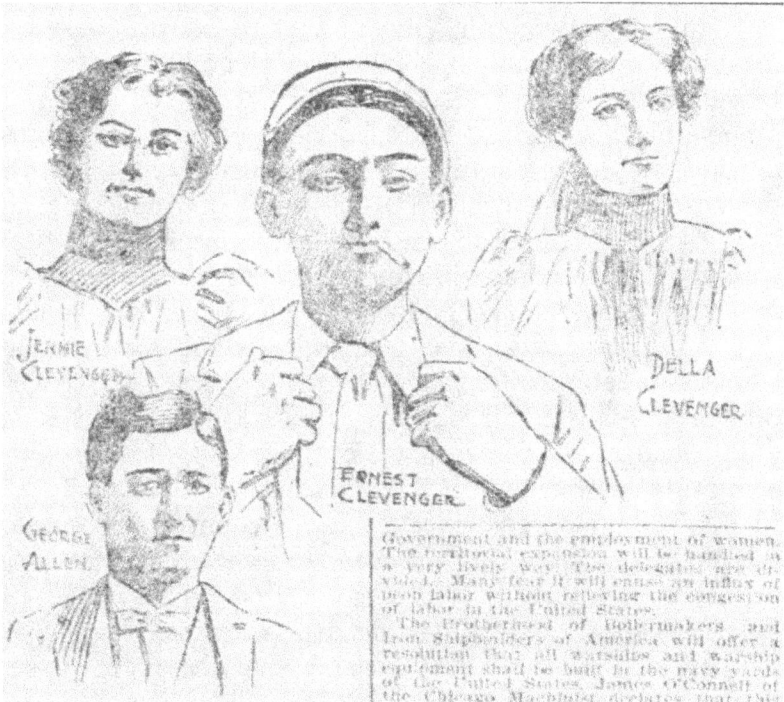

Sketch of the principal actors in the Clevenger shooting. *St. Louis Post Dispatch.*

As Ernest Clevenger fled, several men, including Jerome Clevenger, chased after him, not knowing the extent of the injuries he'd inflicted. Outside the school house, they managed to wrest his pistol from him, but he broke away and escaped. Going back inside, they found George Allen dead and Della gravely wounded with a bullet to the head.

A short distance from the school house, the fugitive stopped at a residence and begged to borrow a pistol, saying he needed it for protection from two robbers who were following him. Supplied with the revolver, he went back to the school house, according to at least one report, and fired a shot at Jennie Clevenger before fleeing again. Pursued by a constable, he turned and fired two shots at the lawman, who promptly retreated.

Two separate posses were put on young Clevenger's trail, and the next morning about 6:00 a.m. he was tracked to the home of his grandfather, John Clevenger, less than a mile from the school house. He was lying by a stove covered with a horse blanket, and as the Clay County sheriff and several deputies closed in, the fugitive raised up and shot himself in the head. Thinking he had inflicted a fatal wound, he lay back down to die, but the ball had only caused a deep flesh wound. When the sheriff roused him moments later, he moaned, "Oh, what have I done? What happened last night?"

Clevenger was put on a train, bound for the Clay County Jail at Liberty. During the trip, Russell Clevenger, brother to Jennie and Della, asked Ernest why he did what he did. "I had my own reason," Clevenger said. "I am sorry I shot Della, but I meant to kill Jennie and your dad, too."

The prisoner was lodged in the county calaboose on the morning of the 9th, and later the same day a coroner's jury charged him with murder in the first degree in George Allen's death. The sheriff and his deputies were on high alert in fear of a lynching that evening, but the night passed without incident. The next morning, Clevenger appeared before a justice of the peace to plead not guilty, and he was remanded without bond to the county jail to await the action of a grand jury.

On the night of December 10, a boisterous mob stormed the county jail with a dummy they'd brought along, dragged it back outside, and hanged it in effigy above the main entrance to the courthouse. The "practical joke" scared both the prisoner and the sheriff almost into an apoplexy, but talk of an actual lynching gradually subsided over the next few days as Della, whom doctors thought at first would surely die, seemed to rally. In addition, both Jerome Clevenger and George Allen's father requested that the law be allowed to take its course.

Ernest Clevenger was officially indicted at the February 1899 term of the Clay County Circuit Court, but the case was continued to the following June term.

In the wee hours of the morning, April 6, Clevenger and three other prisoners made their escape from the Clay County Jail. They pried a lock off with the leg of an iron bed, but it was thought that they also probably had help from the outside. Authorities speculated that Clevenger might be bound for East Tennessee, where he was originally from. He was described as twenty-three years of age, standing five feet and nine inches tall, and weighing 140 pounds. His face was smooth with a scar on the forehead between his eyes. A reward of $100 was offered for his recapture.

Instead of heading to the Volunteer State, Clevenger went back to his nearby Missouri haunts. He was captured on the morning of April 17 near Vibbard, in Ray County, where he had relatives and about ten miles northeast from where he was captured the first time. He was found hiding in a cemetery and was arrested by a local constable. Clay County sheriff John King traveled to Vibbard to take charge of the prisoner and escort him back to Liberty. Clevenger said the reason he didn't get any farther away than he did during his eleven days of freedom was that he kept getting lost in the dark at night and traveling over the same ground he'd already covered.

On April 18, the day after Clevenger was brought back to jail, Della Clevenger died of the wound he had inflicted on her four months earlier. Talk of lynching the prisoner flared again, prompting Clay County deputies to move Clevenger aboard a train to an undisclosed location for temporary safekeeping until the mob fever abated.

At the June term of Clay County Circuit Court, Clevenger applied for and was granted another continuance. The trial finally got underway in November and lasted only two days. After Clevenger pleaded not guilty, his lawyers applied for a change of venue, but the motion was overruled. On November 7, the defense argued its case based on insanity, but the next day the jury found the defendant guilty of first-degree murder. Sentencing was deferred until November 21, when Judge E. J. Broadus pronounced a death sentence by hanging and set the execution date for January 5, 1900. Clevenger's lawyers appealed to the Missouri Supreme Court, and the hanging was postponed.

On May 8, 1900, the high court affirmed the lower court's decision in the Clevenger case, rejecting the defense attorneys' argument that their client should have been granted the requested change of venue. The execution date was reset for June 15.

As the fateful day approached, those sympathetic to Clevenger's insanity plea circulated a petition and forwarded it to Missouri governor Lon Stephens asking for clemency. The petitioners said Clevenger was a "mental and moral degenerate" who was inflamed by whiskey and jealousy and that hanging him would do no good. Stephens, however, declined to intervene and allowed the death sentence to stand.

The condemned man was baptized on June 14 and spent his last full day on earth in consultation with his spiritual advisors. He slept little that night and spent the time writing letters.

He was led from his cell at four o'clock in the morning on June 15. After another consultation with his spiritual advisors in the county collector's office, he said he had made peace with God and was ready to die. He then ate a hearty breakfast and smoked a cigar. The death warrant was read to him, and he was led to the gallows at 5:00 a.m.

Two ministers accompanied him onto the scaffold. Asked, as his arms and legs were strapped, if he had any final words, he said that God was with him, bid farewell to the fifty or so witnesses inside the stockade, and proclaimed, "I ain't worthy of the death I am dying." Then he was dropped through the trap and pronounced dead thirteen minutes later.

20

The Savage Instinct to Kill

The Lynching of Mindu Cowahgee

Mindu Cowahgee had no way of knowing the trouble he was getting into when he decided to break into the Houx Brothers Shoe Store and J. S. Kelley's Jewelry Store in Marshall, Missouri, on the night of March 30, 1900. The *Marshall Republican* reported a few days later that the burglar took two pairs of men's shoes from the shoe store (valued at less than $10) and about $35 worth of gold chains and bracelets from the jewelry store, but Cowahgee ended up paying a much dearer price for the pilfered goods.

He had broken a plate glass window to gain access to the jewelry store and apparently cut himself in the process. The next day, he was arrested in Marshall after a man he'd previously worked for asked him about the suspicious cuts and bruises on his face and neck. When he reacted nervously, a policeman was summoned, and Cowahgee was lodged in the Saline County Jail, where *Republican* editor Percy H. Van Dyke predicted that he would "entertain the inmates…with some of his many adventures."

If Cowahgee regaled the other inmates at the Saline County Jail with stories of his misadventures, he did so for less than a month. On Thursday evening, April 26, as Sheriff Joseph Wilson was herding the inmates into their cells to lock them down for the night, Cowahgee and a black prisoner named John Smith threw Wilson to the floor and took his revolver. Wilson called to his teenage son to bolt the door, but the two men grabbed the boy and slung him out of the way before he could carry out the assignment. Drawn by the commotion, the sheriff's wife, Elizabeth, then appeared on the front steps of the jail to try to block the men's exit, and Cowahgee, carrying the sheriff's revolver, fired the weapon at her. The bullet struck her in the upper left arm, and he and Smith dashed past her to make their escape through the streets of Marshall.

All the deputies that could be spared were quickly put on the escapees' trail, and many citizens, angered by the shooting of the sheriff's wife, joined in the hunt. A reward of $300 was offered for capture of the fugitives, and their descriptions were sent to law officers in surrounding towns.

Smith, who'd recently been convicted of an unknown crime and was awaiting transfer to the Missouri State Penitentiary to serve a ten-year sentence, was described as a "heavy-set, jet black negro." Standing about 5'7" and weighing about 180 pounds, he had "very kinky hair" and was "very shabby" in appearance.

Cowahgee, supposedly a former convict, was variously described as a "Negro," an "Indian," and a "Hindoo," suggesting that he might have been a dark-complexioned native of India. He was "fairly tall," with a medium build, and weighed about 170 pounds.

On Friday morning the 27th, Cowahgee was spotted about two miles east of Marshall, but he fled south into the woods of the Salt Fork River before he could be apprehended. Three hundred men, more determined than ever to catch the fugitive after learning that the doctor attending Mrs. Wilson had been forced to amputate her arm the night before, scoured the timber along the creek, and a bloodhound was also put on the trail. That evening, Cowahgee stole a horse from a farmer living near Napton and inexplicably started riding back toward Marshall. He stopped at the home of Martin Hays and asked for supper. Pretending not to know Cowahgee's identity, Hays invited the fugitive into the house and promptly leveled a shotgun at him as soon as he let his guard down.

Cowahgee was bound hand and foot, brought back to Marshall, and lodged in the city jail late Friday night. With his apprehension, the chase after Smith was virtually abandoned, as it was assumed that he had "already taken flight to other parts."

Mutterings of mob violence were whispered about early on Saturday morning, and Cowahgee was moved about 8:00 a.m. to the county jail, which was considered a more secure facility. Sheriff Wilson once again assumed custody of the prisoner. Soon after the transfer, a large body of men gathered around the jail, but Wilson, urging the crowd to let the law take its course, convinced them to disperse.

Many thought the danger of mob action had passed, but, as the *Republican* noted, "The quiet of the day was but the calm before a storm." Shortly after dark, a mob again started forming at the jail, blocking all the roads and sidewalks that led to the calaboose. "A few half-drunken men stood in front of the jail," the *Republican* continued, "surrounded by a crowd of idle spectators and others who gave their moral support to all talk of lynching."

A prominent citizen addressed the crowd, urging them not to take the law into their own hands, and the sheriff once again appealed to the festering mob, asking them to disband for the sake of his wife's safety. He pointed out that of all offended parties, he and his family had the most reason to want retribution but that it was his and his wife's wish that the law be followed.

The sheriff's appeal quieted the crowd somewhat, but only a few people dispersed. Soon the mob was again clamoring for vengeance and surging in around the guards surrounding the jail. Several other prominent citizens spoke to the unruly crowd, reminding them that the prisoner's offense was not of such enormity that it should result in hanging. They urged the mob to disband, but, in the words of the *Republican*, "their words were wasted."

Several men from one section of the crowd leaped over the fence that surrounded the jail, and they were immediately aped by several more from another section. Had strong action such as firing above the heads of the mob been taken at this moment, opined Van Dyke, the vigilantes might have been turned back, but the sheriff had told his deputies to hold their fire, supposedly because he was concerned that the sounds of gunfire might disturb his recuperating wife. "Affection for wife has proven stronger than sense of duty," the newspaperman lamented.

The vigilantes surged in around the jail with the sheriff and several of his deputies retiring before the advancing horde to the interior. The officers inside the building at first refused the mob's demand that they give up the keys, but then someone outside produced a sledge-hammer and made a start to pound the door. "Only wholesale slaughter of the assailants" could have prevented a lynching at this point, said the *Republican,* and the keys were turned over.

The mob thronged inside and found Cowahgee not in a cell with other prisoners but shackled by himself in a corridor of the jail. The *Republican* described the scene as the condemned man was herded outside:

> Dragged forth to meet the gaze of a thousand on-lookers, the very sight of him seemed to work into a white heat the passions of those who sought his life. Loudly they cried, "Hang him!" and "To the square!"

Offering a similar description, the *Marshall Democrat-News* said that, when the prisoner was brought out with his hands manacled in front of him, "The savage instinct to kill…ran flaming through the excited throng like a wind-fanned fire through dry grass."

Those in the crowd nearest Cowahgee kicked and prodded him, struck him with their fists, or slashed at him with knives as he was dragged by a circuitous route to the courthouse square one block west of the jail. At the southeast corner of the square was a large tree with a branch protruding to the northwest, which the mob meant to use as a makeshift gallows, but no one had a rope to toss over the limb.

Two prominent citizens used the delay in procuring a rope to address the crowd in a last-ditch effort to forestall the lynching, but their words had little effect and no one else spoke up. "The spirit of the masses seemed woefully lacking in any feeling of humanity," said the *Republican* editor, "or any pride in maintaining inviolate the law."

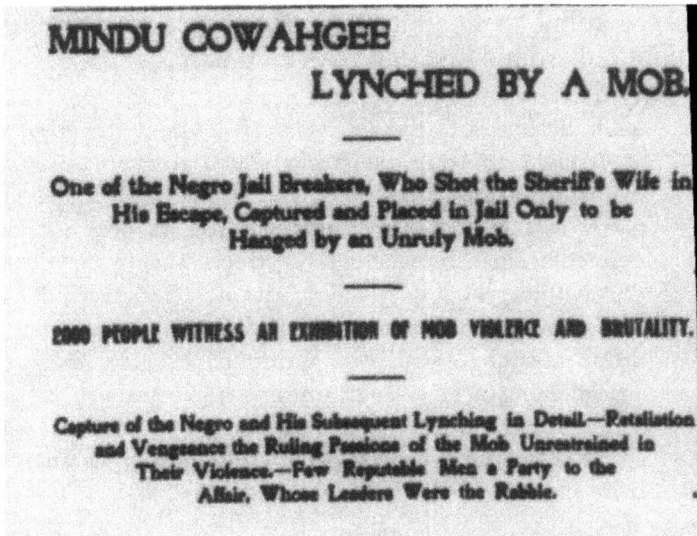

MINDU COWAHGEE
LYNCHED BY A MOB.

——

One of the Negro Jail Breakers, Who Shot the Sheriff's Wife in His Escape, Captured and Placed in Jail Only to be Hanged by an Unruly Mob.

——

2000 PEOPLE WITNESS AN EXHIBITION OF MOB VIOLENCE AND BRUTALITY.

——

Capture of the Negro and His Subsequent Lynching in Detail.—Retaliation and Vengeance the Ruling Passions of the Mob Unrestrained in Their Violence.—Few Reputable Men a Party to the Affair, Whose Leaders Were the Rabble.

Cowahgee lynching headline from the *Marshall Republican.*

Editor Van Dyke reported that Cowahgee asked time to say a prayer when he realized his fate. "Faint from fright, weakened from the cuts and bruises he had received, he asked that the 'Merciful Heavenly Father forgive him of his sins' and those who sought his blood." Turning to one of the leaders of the mob, Cowahgee added, "I have just finished a prayer for mercy for you to the God who is looking down with shame upon you now." The words "struck deep in the conscience of the man," and he "turned back from his course." However, his comrades in lawlessness could not be deterred and "rushed in to take his place."

Continuing the dreadful story, the *Republican* said,

All pleading was in vain. Passion ruled above reason, mob tyranny above law, vengeance above mercy. Cowahgee was allowed a drink just after the rope had been procured, but a few brutes would have refused even this last request, trying to knock the glass from his hands.

Cowahgee's arms were pinioned to his body with rope, according to the Marshall newspaper, and the noose was adjusted around his neck. At 11:20 p.m.,

his body shot into the air, twenty feet above the ground, an awful sight, meeting the gaze of 2,000 people. Many turned from the horrible spectacle. The suspended body, hanging partly in the shadows of newly-leafed maples, but clearly defined against the well lighted streets, gave no evidence of the awfulness of a strangling death. The shackled wrists, which had been drawn upward toward the chest, gradually dropped as life ebbed away. Without a struggle, save a slight straightening as the body grew limp, Cowahgee died, the rope turning the gaze of his helpless head upon those below, some of whom were exultant in the accomplishment and consummation of their illegal and criminal desires.

The body was cut down at 12:10 Sunday morning, and then began "the usual morbid scenes," according to the *Democrat-News*, including a mad scramble "to photograph the distorted face by flash-light" and a rush to retrieve "bits of the rope as grewsome keepsakes."

A coroner's jury was impaneled almost immediately after the body was cut down. The inquest determined, predictably enough, that Mindu Cowahgee "came to his death at the hands of a mob unknown to the jury." The body was removed to an undertaker's office right after the inquest and buried after daybreak in a potter's field at the county farm.

Editor Van Dyke begged to differ with the verdict of the coroner's inquest. The lynching was a travesty of justice and an affront to civilization, he declared in the next issue of the *Republican*, and it was made doubly so because the assault on Mrs. Wilson was not a crime for which anyone would normally receive the death penalty. The jury's negligence of duty in reaching its verdict only compounded the tragedy. The mob was undisguised and all faces clearly visible beneath the glare of the street lights; yet the jury claimed not to know the identity of any of the lawbreakers. In addition, the jury failed even to interview any witnesses, despite the fact that 2,000 people saw the lynching. Van Dyke concluded that the only reasonable inference to be drawn was that most of the jury must have been among the mob. No doubt he knew this to be the case but discreetly chose to imply it rather than state it directly.

Although Van Dyke roundly condemned the mob, he resented reports that came from outside Marshall in the wake of the lynching that the people of the town had taken the law into their own hands to avenge a crime. In the following week's issue of the *Republican*, Van Dyke declared that the leaders of the mob that had hanged Cowahgee in no way represented "the people" of Marshall. "One of the leaders…," he said, "was educated in the reform school, another received training in the state penitentiary and unsavory reputations were carried by others who were in the lead."

While seeming to defend the people of Marshall, Van Dyke was actually censuring them, because he said the fact that the leaders of the mob did not represent the people (and some did not even live in Marshall) only exacerbated the people's sin of omission in not stopping the lynching.

21

Daring to Curse a White Boy

The Lynching of Louis Wright

When young black men were lynched by white mobs during the late 1800s and early 1900s, the initial reaction among the white majority and in the press was usually to justify the extralegal act by asserting that the black man got what he deserved. This was especially the case if the lynching victim had been accused of murdering a white person or assaulting a white woman. But even the lynching of a black man charged with a less serious crime rarely brought a public outcry.

Take the case of Louis Wright, a twenty-one-year-old member of a traveling minstrel show, who was lynched in New Madrid, Missouri, on the night of February 16, 1902. A fight had broken out the night before between the white audience and the minstrels during their performance at the local opera house, and initial reports of the affair said Wright had been the main instigator of the riot and that several white people had been hit by gunfire during the melee.

As more details "were allowed to come out," however, a few newspapers, primarily non-Missouri newspapers, began to question the automatic assumption that Louis Wright "had it coming." A fuller account of the lynching, declared the *Independence (KS) Daily Reporter* three days after the incident, "shows that the minstrels were not the only ones to blame by any means." To those of us today who care to familiarize ourselves with the details of the affair, the *Daily Reporter*'s observation seems like a statement of the obvious. But many in white society around the turn of the twentieth century had a hard time seeing the obvious.

Louis Wright was a singer of "considerable local note" in his hometown of Ottawa, Kansas, before going on the road around 1900 with Richard and Pringle's famous Georgia Minstrels. As a minstrel performer, he developed a reputation as a "homely colored man with a fine tenor voice" and also played the trombone. Off stage, according to at least one source, he was known as a belligerent sort or at least as a person who wouldn't back down from a fight. The *Coffeyville (KS) Weekly Journal* claimed, for instance, that Wright got into a scuffle at the local auditorium during the minstrels' January 1902 appearance in Coffeyville and pulled a knife on a stagehand.

Promotional poster for the Georgia Minstrels. *Courtesy Library of Congress.*

About a month later, the Georgia Minstrels arrived in New Madrid by train on the snowy morning of Saturday, February 15. In the afternoon, the black performers gave a street parade, and some of the local white boys taunted the "flashily dressed" minstrels with gibes as they marched through the downtown area. After the parade ended, Wright and one or two of the other performers walked back to the opera house together, and, as they passed the courthouse, two young white men started throwing hard, slush-packed snowballs at them. When the young black men told them to quit, the local toughs responded by hurling insults as well as more snowballs at the minstrels. Growing angry, Wright turned and cursed the white boys, calling one of the them a "dirty son of a bitch." The town marshal showed up just in time to avert further trouble, advising the white boys to go home and the minstrels to stay off the streets.

That evening, a large crowd packed the opera house in New Madrid for the minstrel performance, and a number of boys and young men, including those who had clashed with the minstrels on the street earlier in the day, took seats at the front of the auditorium near the stage. As one of the black performers later recalled, the local youth were still angry that "a nigger had dared to curse a white boy," and they wanted to find him, take him out, and whip him.

The show had barely begun when some of the young white men started making wisecracks about the performers, and the minstrels promptly replied in kind. The banter seemed good-natured at first, but it soon turned ugly. The remarks, loud enough to be heard throughout the auditorium, became more and more personal as the performance progressed, and "jeers, catcalls and hisses punctuated the entertainment," according to a special report to the *St. Louis Republic*. "Sentimental ballads were received with laughter; the funny gags and jokes brought forth groans. Some of the minstrels made no effort to please and frequently addressed personal remarks to members of the audience."

Some of the older men in the audience tried to get the

"thoughtless youths" to break off the escalating war of words but to no avail. Just as the performance closed and while most of the audience was still in the building, about a half dozen young white men tried to charge the stage. Rushing up some steps through a narrow passageway that led onto the stage, they grabbed a black man named Shields at the top of the steps, thinking he was the one who had cursed the white boys in the afternoon. They turned him loose when somebody pulled out a revolver and fired a shot.

All accounts of the melee that appeared in white newspapers across the country, including the special report to the *Republic*, asserted that the first shot came from one of the black performers on the stage. But even the two local newspapers, the *New Madrid Southeast Missourian* and the *New Madrid Weekly Record*, could not agree on the exact details. And one the minstrels, writing for the *Indianapolis Freeman* a couple of weeks later, claimed that none of the young black men even had a handgun.

After the first gunshot, the place erupted into chaos, said the *Republic* correspondent. Suddenly, "half a dozen pistols were being fired at random by the negroes and white men. Panic ensued in the hall, and men, women and children rushed pell-mell from the building, screaming and crying."

In all, about twenty shots rang out. At least one minstrel and one white man received minor wounds, while several others had close calls, with bullets passing through their clothes or whizzing by their heads. The older white men who'd been trying to calm things down from the beginning finally got the shooters to cease fire, and the black men made their escape out a side door and took refuge in their railroad car, which was parked on a side track nearby.

A mob of whites surrounded the car, but the crowd dispersed after local law officers arrived and placed the minstrels under arrest. Taken to jail and questioned, all of them denied firing any shots or knowing who did, and no weapon was found on any of them. Placed behind bars, the young black men, about twenty-four in number, spent the night crammed into a damp cell with standing room only.

Outside, in the streets of New Madrid, things settled down for the night, but the next day groups of men collected on the corners discussing the shooting affray at the opera house the night before and plotting vigilante action. Meanwhile, throughout the day on Sunday, the prisoners were taken one by one from the jail to the courthouse across the yard for interrogation before a special jury, composed of thirty of the town's "best citizens," which had been called to investigate the shooting. Sheriff Bentley Stone announced to one or more of the minstrels as he escorted them to the hearing, "I can't protect you niggers any longer. You must tell who fired the shot; if not, I leave you to whatever fate these gentlemen may decide."

Under an intense "sweating," one or more of the minstrels revealed that Louis Wright was the person who had cursed the white boy on Saturday afternoon. Most newspaper accounts said Wright was also identified as the man who fired from the stage, but the minstrel whose account appeared in the *Indianapolis Freeman* said such an identification did not come from Wright's fellow performers. Two young white men told the jury of having seen a revolver in Wright's pocket while he was standing near the opera house on Saturday afternoon, but the unidentified *Freeman* letter writer characterized the testimony as "a malicious lie."

In any case, the identification was good enough for the would-be lynchers. Late that night, Sunday, February 16, five masked men marched to the jail. The small mob overpowered Sheriff Stone and his jailer, took the keys, and held the two men prisoner while one of the vigilantes went upstairs and took Wright from his cell, either at gunpoint or, as his fellow minstrel later said, under the ruse that the jury was still in session and that Wright was needed to give a further statement.

Even if trickery was used to get Wright out of the cell, he quickly realized his fate, and, as he was marched downstairs, he pled for his life. But in vain.

The five vigilantes dragged him outside, where they were joined by forty or fifty additional men. The mob took Wright to a big elm tree along Big Prairie Road (i.e. Kingshighway) just north of the railroad tracks on the edge of town. They strung him up to a limb of the tree in front of a black family's home and left him hanging.

The body was viewed by hundreds of people the next morning, before Sheriff Stone cut it down. Later on Monday, a coroner's jury found that Wright had come to his death by hanging by parties unknown. The rest of the minstrels were released the same day.

Before they boarded a train out of town, a local reporter interviewed their manager, George A. Treyser. He attributed the tragic affair to the fact that his troupe had lately toured in the North, where they'd been treated as equals, and some of his men had gotten the "swell-head." Treyser said he tried to warn his men that folks in this section of the country "would not tolerate negro equality."

On Thursday, Wright's body, minus the rings that had been taken off the fingers, was placed in a box and shipped to his mother in Chicago, where the family had resettled.

Interviewed a couple of weeks later in Minnesota, Treyser admitted that Wright had fired a single shot from the stage but only after some of the white men starting shooting at the feet of another minstrel in an effort to scare him.

Even if Wright was guilty of more than just "cursing a white boy," one thing seems clear: the *Independence Daily Reporter* was correct in saying that Wright and his fellow minstrels were "not the only ones to blame by any means" for his lynching. Perhaps the main mistake the minstrels made, as the *Daily Reporter* also concluded, was their "bad judgment in attempting to give an entertainment in a thoroughly wild and wooly Missouri town."

Too Many Wives

The Vigilante Murder of a "Sanctified" Preacher

About 1900, D. M. Malone, a former Methodist minister who'd recently embraced the holiness movement sweeping across the country at the time, started preaching his newfound gospel of Christian perfection in the Little River area of northwest Pemiscot County, Missouri. The holiness movement emphasized union with God or "sanctification," and those who claimed to have achieved such a state often considered themselves accountable only to heaven. Malone soon learned that many of his neighbors were resistant to his unorthodox religious beliefs, but what really riled them up was his unconventional lifestyle and his mistreatment of his wife. Rev. Malone might have thought he was following the laws of God, but it was his flouting of the laws of man that ended up getting him killed.

Sometime around the beginning of 1903, Malone left his wife, Alice, and their children at home while he took a trip into Arkansas and Mississippi. When he returned, he surprised Alice by bringing a good-looking "grass widow" named Mary Friel home to live with them as their "housekeeper," claiming that Alice was incompetent to attend to her household duties. Some reports at the time suggested that Malone had picked Mary up during his trip south, but twenty-six-year-old Mary "Molly" Friel was, in fact, the estranged wife of James Friel from the Portageville vicinity of neighboring New Madrid County. The forty-six-year-old preacher had made Mary's acquaintance while proselytizing in that area prior to his trip, and the pair made the journey south together.

THE REVEREND D. M. MALONE.

D. M. Malone, a "sanctified" preacher. From the *St. Louis Republic.*

Alice, who had been married to Malone for almost twenty-five years, objected to the new living arrangement, but the preacher said that Mary shared his holiness fervor and was indispensable to his evangelical work. Malone and the young woman tried to convert Alice to the sanctified sect as well, but the thirty-eight-year-old Mrs. Malone "could not believe their doctrine," according to her later story, and she also greatly objected to her husband having "another wife."

Malone and Mary continued traveling and preaching together, although they largely avoided the New Madrid County area where she was from, having incurred the hostility of the people in that vicinity with their "holiness" meetings and their growing intimacy. When they were home, though, Malone's wife still stood in the way of their "entire sanctification." Their attempts to convert Alice having proved unsuccessful, they started plotting to put her aside. Accusing her of being crazy and a danger to other people, they even resorted to tying her to a bed with leather thongs.

Meanwhile, some of Alice Malone's neighbors rose to her defense, and "an internecine war" developed between D. M. Malone and his "Holiness" allies versus an "Anti-Holiness-Malone" faction led "by no one in particular and everyone in general," according to the *Caruthersville Twice-A-Week Democrat*. The mounting tension came to a head on Saturday night, April 25, when some of the anti-holiness crowd fired several shots into the Malone house in an attempt to "whitecap" the preacher and his paramour.

Instead of backing down, Malone responded by having his wife arrested on an insanity charge, claiming she'd tried to kill someone. A constable brought Alice to Caruthersville on Tuesday, April 28, and lodged her in the Pemiscot County Jail.

Some people doubted the charge of insanity almost from the beginning. Alice was not assigned a cell but given the run of the jail, and when a *Twice-A-Week Democrat* reporter interviewed her shortly after her arrival, he concluded, "She may be insane, but she don't talk like it; she may be desperate, but she does not look nor act that way."

Alice told the newspaperman that, if she was crazy, it was because she had had enough trouble to make her so. Although appearing not to be vindictive toward anyone, she related the story of her husband's installation of Mary Friel as a "housekeeper" in the Malone home and the pair's mistreatment of her.

Alice Malone's arrest so inflamed many of her neighbors that P. C. Hill, a justice of the peace in Little River Township, felt something had to be done and took matters into his own hands. He swore out a warrant against Malone for wife abandonment, and gave it to Constable W. J.

Mooneyhan of Wardell to serve. When Mooneyhan showed up at the Malone residence on Wednesday the 29th, however, Malone greeted him with a Winchester in his hands and two revolvers strapped around his waist. Defying arrest, the preacher said he "was not living under the laws of man but under the laws of grace." He added that, if anybody "fooled" with him, he would get three or four more women to live with him.

TOO MANY WIVES.

A Sanctified Parson Creates All Kinds of Trouble in Little River Neighborhood.

OPENLY DEFIED OFFICER.

Caruthersville Twice-A-Week Democrat sums up what led to Malone's lynching.

Sizing Malone up as a desperate man, Mooneyhan decided not to press the issue but instead went back to Justice Hill to report the incident. Uncertain what to do, Hill traveled to Caruthersville to consult with county authorities, and he and the other officers decided to charge Malone and Mary Friel with adultery. County prosecutor L. L. Collins issued the writ, and Hill took it back to Wardell for Mooneyhan to serve.

Constable Mooneyhan rounded up a posse of about eighteen men and set out to serve the warrant on Friday, May

1, 1903. The posse arrived at the Malone place late that night and surrounded the house. They waited for dawn before announcing themselves and demanding the surrender of Malone and his distaff partner in holiness. The preacher again refused, poking the barrel of his Winchester through an opening in the front wall of the house and warning Mooneyhan and his deputies not to come inside the fence surrounding the home. While Mooneyhan and Malone continued to parley, one of the deputies sneaked up and set a fire beneath the rear of the house. When the flames started to break through the floor, Malone, realizing he was going to be burned out, volunteered to surrender if he and Mary would be protected. Mooneyhan promised to protect them, the fire was quickly doused, and Malone and Mrs. Friel were taken into custody.

After the surrender, the prisoners were taken to Justice Hill, who bound them over to the Pemiscot County Circuit Court. Most of the posse was dismissed, while Mooneyhan and two deputies he retained as guards escorted the prisoners to Mooneyhan's house at Wardell, where the constable planned to spend the night before making the trip to Caruthersville the next morning.

On Saturday night, as Mooneyhan, his wife, the two guards, and several other visitors in the Mooneyhan home were sitting around the fireside listening to Mary Friel and the "sin-proof parson" discuss their faith, Malone seemed restless and kept saying he expected to be lynched before daylight. Mooneyhan tried to reassure him but with little success.

Shortly before midnight, a noise came from the front steps, and Mooneyhan went to the door with his pistol in hand to check on it. Opening the door, he was faced by four or five heavily armed men standing on the porch. One or more of the intruders spoke, but nobody inside the house could make out the words. Then Mooneyhan was heard to reply, "No, boys, I can't do it. I've given my word, and, if necessary, I'll give my life."

The man standing nearest Mooneyhan promptly shot the constable in the head, and he fell back in the door dead. The sound of the shot and the sight of Mooneyhan collapsing threw those inside the house into confusion, with Malone and Molly Friel making a dash for freedom.

Charging into the house, the mob caught Malone in a hallway, threw him down, and yanked him out to the porch, where they shot him. They then dragged him by his heels about 200 yards to the bank of the Little River, emptying their revolvers into his body as they went along.

In the meantime, Mary escaped out the back door of the house and scaled a fence into an orchard, where she climbed up in an apple tree to hide. When the mob returned to the house and demanded that Mary be turned over to them, they were told that she had escaped. After a hasty search of the house, the vigilantes made no further effort to find Mary but instead mounted their horses and galloped away, heading north.

The mob was thought to have come from New Madrid County. The next day, two families living about three miles north of Wardell reported that about eighteen to twenty riders had galloped past their house going south about 10:00 p.m. Saturday night and a similar number of horseman passed on a dead run going north about 1:00 a.m. Sunday. Other estimates placed the number of men composing the mob as few as eight.

Mary Friel climbed out of her tree early Sunday morning, and later that morning one of the deputies who'd been detailed to help guard her took her to Caruthersville to lodge her in the county jail and to report the murders of Mooneyhan and Malone. After Mary was brought in, she was placed in a cell, and Alice Malone, forced to relinquish her limited freedom, was assigned a separate cell to keep her and the other woman apart.

On Monday, May 4, Pemiscot County sheriff J. A. "Chip" Franklin went out to the scene of the crime to investigate the murders and found Mooneyhan's and

Malone's neighbors gathered at the constable's residence for the burial of the two victims. Franklin went back to Caruthersville that evening, reporting that he'd obtained several clues as to the identity of the mob.

The next day, May 5, the sheriff went back out, armed with the intelligence he'd gained the day before. Venturing into New Madrid County, he returned that night via train from Portageville with six prisoners in tow. Their names were W. T. "Ruff" Nichols, Jeff "Press" Nichols, Dave Disher, J. C. Price, Bob GoDair, and Ed Chitty.

Interviewed at the county jail on May 7, Mary Friel was asked whether Malone compelled her to live with him. She didn't directly answer the question but said she was afraid to disregard his requests. She showed the reporter an undated letter Malone had written to her that she said showed his disposition toward her. It read,

> Dear Sister—I am true to you, and if you are true to your word, come to me. If you do not come to me, I will come to you, and our days will be short. Send me the picture you had taken at Piggott, Ark., so that it may be placed over the bullet hole that pierces my heart if I am killed. Yours in Christ,
>   D. M. Malone.

From her adjoining cell, Alice Malone overheard some of the reporter's conversation with Mary Friel and went into a rage, berating both her husband and Mary. Asked whether she could not forgive her husband now that he was dead, she shook her head. She said she couldn't forgive him because of the way he and Mary had mistreated her and because "the trouble he got into with that woman" was the cause of Mr. Mooneyhan's death. Despite her anger toward her dead husband, Alice mostly blamed Mary for ruining "a good man."

Soon after the reporter left, Alice was declared sane and released. She returned to her home in Pemiscot County, where she continued to live for several years. How long Mary Friel was held in jail or the final disposition of her case is uncertain.

A week or two after Sheriff Franklin arrested the first batch of suspects, another six men were rounded up: George Ward, Will Nicholas, Lonnie Keith, Charles Taylor, Martin Welch, and Fred Ensley.

Most of the twelve men arrested were from the Portageville vicinity, where Mary Friel had previously lived with her husband. Portageville was about ten miles upstream from Wardell on the Little River, and several of the ringleaders of the mob lived near a sawmill on the river. This was the same vicinity that Malone and Mary had been run out of a few months earlier because of their scandalous dalliance and their holiness preaching.

Some of the arrested men were even said to have been among Constable Mooneyhan's posse. They'd helped arrest Malone on Saturday morning and then returned that night to kill him.

Preliminary hearings for the twelve suspects began in the Pemiscot County Circuit Court on May 20, 1903. Five of the men; Ruff Nichols, Dave Disher, J. C. Price, George Ward, and Ed Chitty; were indicted for murder, while the other seven were released without charges. However, the investigation continued, and several additional men from the Portageville area, including John "Shorty" Adams and Martin Snider, were arrested, while charges against all the previously indicted men except Chitty were dropped.

Only Chitty, Adams, and Snider ultimately went on trial, in December of 1904 for the killing of D. M. Malone. They were charged with first-degree murder but were convicted of second-degree and sentenced to fifteen years apiece in the Missouri State Penitentiary. They were admitted to the state prison in Jefferson City on December 27, 1904. They appealed their convictions to the Missouri Supreme Court, but they had no representation and filed no bill of exceptions. So the appeal was quickly rejected and the verdict of the lower court upheld. However, the sentences of all three men were commuted by the Missouri governor after they had served only about five years.

Shorty Adams, who'd been involved in an attempted insurance fraud against the Modern Woodmen of America a couple of years before the Malone lynching, was beat to death with a pool cue at Portageville in October of 1910 not long after he'd been pardoned. "Thus Shorty's eventful career is ended here," concluded the *New Madrid Southeast Missourian*.

"Would Have Done a White Man
the Same Way"

The Lynching of Kidnapper Robert Pettigrew

Early Friday morning, May 12, 1905, Robert "Bob" Pettigrew (aka Tom Witherspoon) showed up at the home of Fred Hess, about three miles below Belmont, Missouri, on the Mississippi River, armed with a rifle and a double-barrel shotgun. Hess was an ex-Mississippi County judge and a former state representative, while Pettigrew was a young black man, about twenty-seven years old, who had just been released a month earlier from the Missouri State Penitentiary after serving three years for assaulting his wife with intent to kill. Hess had been a witness against Pettigrew, and the ex-con felt Hess and the state owed him for the time he'd spent behind bars. Pettigrew figured that, even if Hess had to pay with his personal funds, the state would reimburse him.

Things didn't quite work out that way.

Pettigrew accosted the fifty-five-year-old Hess at the barn and demanded $600. Hess didn't take the demand seriously until the desperate Pettigrew pointed his shotgun at him and threatened to blow his brains out if he didn't produce the money in a hurry. Hess said he didn't have that kind of money on the place; so Pettigrew told him he'd have to go to town and get it. He ordered Hess to hitch up his horse and buggy and also to get a saddle horse ready.

Hess's young wife, twenty-eight-year-old Emma Prince Hess, was fixing breakfast when she noticed the unusual goings-on outside and saw her husband hitching up the buggy. Stepping outside to investigate, she was met by her husband, who whispered to her what was happening but told her to act as if nothing was wrong. Pettigrew ordered the couple to quit whispering, and Mrs. Hess went inside.

As soon as Hess got the horses ready, Pettigrew told him to fetch his wife, who would serve as a hostage while Hess went into town for the money. Mrs. Hess came back outside and got into the buggy as directed, and her husband climbed into the driver's seat beside her. Pettigrew mounted the other horse and followed closely behind as Hess started the buggy toward Belmont.

Hess whispered the full story to his wife as they rode along. Pettigrew, whom Mrs. Hess knew as "Bob," stayed right behind the buggy with his horse's nose almost against it. His rifle was slung across his back, and the double-barrel shotgun lay across the saddle with both hammers cocked. Fearing the gun might go off, Judge Hess asked him to uncock it. "Never mind," Pettigrew replied nonchalantly. "I'll keep it cocked. It won't go off unless I want it to."

A couple of times during the trip to town when Hess's horse broke into a trot, Pettigrew galloped up and, thrusting the shotgun against the buggy, told the driver to slow down. "We'll get there time enough without trotting."

At the edge of Belmont, Pettigrew ordered Hess to halt the buggy, get down, and unlatch a gate that opened onto a trail running alongside a railroad track to the Negro Baptist Church. After entering through the gate, Hess drove along the track past a barn to the back side of the church, where the pastor's house, "a three-room negro cabin," was located.

Bob ordered "Miss Prince," as he called her, into the house and told Hess to go to town and get the money. Taking out a cheap pocket watch, the kidnapper glanced at the timepiece and told the judge he'd give him an hour and half. If Hess wasn't back with the money by that time, Pettigrew warned, "There'll be a dead woman here when you do come."

After Hess hurried away in the buggy, Pettigrew hid his horse behind the house and then went inside where Mrs. Hess was. He ordered her into an adjoining room, where an elderly black lady was, and Mrs. Hess talked to the old woman about everyday matters like sewing, trying to pretend she was just paying a social call. Through the open door between the two rooms, Mrs. Hess could see Bob pacing the floor with one of his weapons pointed in her direction.

Meanwhile, Judge Hess reached Belmont but was able to round up only about $60 on the spur of the moment. He sent the money back to Pettigrew by the pastor of the black church, the Rev. Perry Thurman, and Hess or someone else also sent word to Charleston, the seat of Mississippi County, that his wife had been kidnapped. Then he raced toward Columbus, Kentucky, just across the Mississippi River, to come up with the rest of the $600.

Inside the parsonage, Pettigrew's pacing grew more frantic as the last minutes of the allotted hour and a half ticked away. Just three minutes before the time was to expire, Mrs. Hess saw Rev. Thurman running toward the house with a handful of money.

Meeting Thurman at the front door, Pettigrew let the parson in and took the money but gave it back as soon as he saw the puny amount. "You go tell Judge Hess I said $600, and I've got to have all of it in paper. I'll give him half an hour more to get it here, and if it isn't here then, there'll be a dead white woman on the floor in yonder."

After Thurman hurried away, Bob came to the door separating the two rooms and called Mrs. Hess to the threshold but did not enter her room.

"Yes, Bob, what do you want?" she said.

"I want to talk to you, Miss Prince."

"All right, Bob" she said with a smile, trying not to show fear.

Pettigrew talked to her for several minutes, but he was mumbling so badly that Mrs. Hess could hardly understand him. One thing she was able make out was Bob's wish that she tell her husband he would get his money back.

She said she would, but she worried that Bob might kill her.

Prince Hess, whose kidnapping led to lynching of Pettigrew. *Los Angeles Herald.*

"I ain't going to hurt you, Miss Prince," he said, "if the judge brings the money."

Mrs. Hess returned to her seat, and Pettigrew went back to walking the floor in the other room. After a while, the judge's wife heard her captor nervously fiddling with his shotgun, lifting and dropping the hammers, then breaking it open and closing it back.

Meanwhile, when Judge Hess reached Columbus, he quickly raised the $600 but also spread the word of what the money was for. A posse of angry Kentuckians, led by Columbus city marshal Bob Zimmerman, followed him back to Belmont bent on capturing the kidnapper, but Hess cautioned them and the local Missourians who joined them to stay back until the money was delivered.

As the additional half hour was about to expire, Mrs. Hess looked out the window and saw men with guns surrounding two sides of the house and Parson Thurman again running toward the house with a larger wad of bills than before. Bob let the preacher in the door and took the money. Thurman was just explaining why Hess himself had not delivered it when Pettigrew also spotted the men surrounding the house.

Making a dash for freedom, he mounted his horse and galloped away. The men surrounding the house held their fire at first for fear of hitting Mrs. Hess, but as soon as Pettigrew was safely away from the house, they opened fire. Pettigrew returned fire as he made his escape.

Deputy Sheriff R. S. Paris and about twelve armed deputies arrived from Charleston on a switch engine to join the Kentucky posse, and in the pursuit that followed, Pettigrew was forced to abandon his horse and flee on foot into the swamps below Belmont. Bloodhounds were brought in, and the searchers located the fugitive in a deserted shanty about five o'clock Friday afternoon.

Pettigrew took refuge in the attic, and after a brief parley with the posse, he threw down the $600, apparently hoping that giving the money back might persuade his pursuers to retire from the fray. When they didn't, he threatened to shoot the first one who came through the door. After trying unsuccessfully to burn the fugitive out, the posse made a charge on the house. In trying to maneuver into a firing position, Pettigrew fell from the loft, and he was surrounded and arrested before he could rise.

Deputy Paris and Marshal Zimmerman took the captive back to Belmont to lodge him in the local calaboose, but before he could be locked up, a mob appeared and demanded that he be turned over to them. At least some of the lawmen tried to resist the vigilante horde at first. Deputy Paris, in particular, twice cut the rope with which the mob was going to hang Pettigrew, but as the crowd grew to about 200 men and their mood coarsened, the deputy decided that discretion was the better part of valor.

The vigilantes took Pettigrew to the public square and, using a rope taken from a child's swing, strung him up to a tree (or a telephone pole, as one report said). Some of the mob also reportedly fired into the body after Pettigrew was hanging.

Upon learning of the mob violence, Missouri governor Joseph Folk swiftly condemned it, saying such outlawry would not be tolerated in his state. He instructed his attorney general, Herbert Hadley, to act in conjunction with the Mississippi County prosecuting attorney to insure that the lynchers were brought to justice. Hadley himself added that there was no excuse for the posse taking Pettigrew out and hanging him, especially since he was not accused of "the usual negro crime."

A Mississippi County grand jury was scheduled for May 25 to investigate the lynching, but, despite the calls from state officials like Governor Folk to prosecute the members of the mob, very little was ever done to bring the vigilantes to justice. Some Missouri newspapers pointed out that most of the mob had come from Kentucky, and several even published indignant editorials justifying the vigilante action and castigating the governor for his tough stance against the mob.

The *Jackson (MO) Herald*, for instance, said the law recognized motive and intent and that "murder was the intention of this negro." Had not Judge Hess done exactly what Pettigrew wanted, the villain "would have killed Hess and his wife and baby." The citizens who hanged Pettigrew "would have done a white man the same way."

Like nearly every other newspaper story in the immediate wake of the lynching, the *Herald* editorial included the false assertion that Pettigrew took the Hess child hostage at the same time he kidnapped the boy's parents. Interviewed a week or so after the lynching, Mrs. Hess made clear that her child was left at home during her ordeal. Asked whether she thought Pettigrew should have been lynched, she said, "Not for what he did to me."

But none of the mob bothered to ask Miss Prince her opinion.

Chapter 24

I Hope I Burn Forever

Murder of the Filley Family and Hanging of Albert Filley

The *Cameron (MO) Daily Observer* reported on December 17, 1907, that Mrs. Albert Filley, living five miles southeast of Cameron, had been kicked in the head by a horse on the 14th and was unconscious for two days before starting to show signs of life on the 16th. Discovering her lying senseless in a stable full of horses, her husband, "completely overwhelmed," had run to a neighbor's home for help, and the neighbor had come and carried the unconscious woman to her house.

As future events and testimony would reveal, that's not quite the way it happened.

On Saturday morning, December 21, exactly a week after Mrs. Filley had supposedly been kicked in the head by a horse, the Filley neighborhood southeast of Cameron was horrorstricken when they awoke to learn that Albert Filley had killed his wife, his little girl, and his brother. He'd also tried to kill his sister-in-law, but she had escaped in her nightclothes at four o'clock in the morning and raced to the neighboring home of J. W. Chaffin, the same man whose aid Filley had sought a week earlier, to give the alarm.

Local constable Frank Stream was summoned, and he and a small posse of men from the neighborhood surrounded the Filley home. Thirty-two-year-old Albert Filley stepped out onto the front porch, and Stream, covering him with a revolver, arrested him without further incident.

Inside the Filley home, the neighbors found Albert's twenty-nine-year-old wife, Fannie, lying dead in her bed. Her skull was crushed from several blows to the head, and a bloody hammer, the apparent murder weapon, was found nearby. Lying partly beneath the bed was the body of seven-year-old Dolly Filley, the couple's daughter, and her head, like that of her mother, showed evidence of having been struck with a blunt instrument.

Clay Filley, who'd been staying with his younger brother to help out with the chores ever since Fannie had been injured, was found dead on the floor near the doorway separating Albert and Fannie's bedroom from the room where Clay and his family had been sleeping. He'd apparently died of a single gunshot wound, as no other marks of violence were found on his body. Clay's wife, thirty-six-year-old Elsie, had been knocked senseless, but she'd regained consciousness and, while still bleeding from her head wound, escaped to the Chaffin residence, taking her infant child with her.

The marshal of Cameron soon arrived to help guard the prisoner until Caldwell County authorities could get there. Cameron was located in Clinton County, but the Filley home was on the Caldwell County side of the road that separated the two counties. After Caldwell County sheriff Frank Parker arrived, he took charge of the prisoner and took him to the county calaboose at Kingston almost twenty miles away.

Meanwhile, the bodies were left lying as they'd been found until the coroner arrived from Kingston. He called an inquest on Saturday, the same day the tragedy happened, and the jury concluded that the three victims had come to their deaths at the hands of Albert Filley. After the inquest, the prisoner was officially charged with murder and held for trial without bail.

The next day, funeral services were held at the Filley home for Fannie, Dolly, and Clay Filley, and the bodies of all three were then taken to McDaniel Cemetery a couple of miles east of Cameron on present-day Old Highway 36 for burial.

Seeking an explanation for the incomprehensible

murders, some people in the Filley neighborhood mentioned that Albert had been suffering severe pain from a felon on one of his fingers, which is partly why Clay and his family had been staying with Albert to help him out. It was theorized that either the pain itself had driven Albert to his maniacal deed or else he'd drunk himself crazy seeking relief from the pain.

Recuperating at a neighbor's home, Elsie Filley soon rallied enough to relate the story of the crime in more detail. She said her husband, Clay, was sitting up with Fannie when his brother suddenly burst into the room without provocation about 4:00 a.m. and shot him with a revolver. The wounded Clay sprang up, and the two men wrestled over the pistol. Albert Finney finally broke loose and fled outdoors, while Clay went to the kitchen, where his wife and child were sleeping. He awakened Elsie and told her what had happened. She and Clay barricaded the house to keep Albert out, but he soon returned with a hammer and a stick of wood and smashed the glass in the kitchen door. Elsie and Clay fought at the door with Albert to keep him out, and he soon retreated to a well and started pumping water. By now, Clay Filley was so weak from his bullet wound that he sank to the floor dying. When Elsie heard her crazed brother-in-law returning to the house, she grabbed a bottle of carbolic acid and threw it on him, but it didn't keep him from forcing his way into the house. Albert struck Elsie down with a blow from the stick of wood and stalked into his wife's room. As Filley went to work smashing in the brains of his wife and daughter, Elsie revived enough to snatch her baby girl from bed and dash out of the house toward the J. W. Chaffin place.

A newspaperman called at the county jail in Kingston on Sunday, December 22, to get Albert Filley's side of the story. Still suffering from the facial burns inflicted by the acid Elsie had thrown on him and from bruises about the head he'd received from his brother, Albert spoke to the reporter in the presence of Sheriff Parker. Filley showed little emotion except that he seemed pleased after he was erroneously informed that his sister-in-law was dead, and when he launched into his tale, he told a much different story than the version Elsie had given.

Albert said that he, Clay, and Elsie were all sitting up with Fannie on the night in question. Near morning, he went outside to check on his chickens. When he returned after about thirty minutes, he found his wife and child lying dead, and Elsie immediately attacked him with a wooden club. Clay, also armed with a club, promptly joined his wife in the assault. After fighting the pair a short while, Albert managed to get the revolver he'd taken with him to the chicken coop out of his pocket and shoot his brother. Despite being shot, Clay continued fighting, and he and Elsie knocked Albert down. Clay collapsed about the same time, and while Albert lay stunned on the floor, Elsie escaped.

The prisoner denied having assaulted his wife in the barn a week earlier in an attempt to kill her, as nearly everyone now suspected. He said he and Fannie had never had any trouble, and he could give no reason why Clay and Elsie had killed his wife either, because they, too, never had any trouble with her.

The next day, Monday the 23rd, the revolver was found hidden in a well on the Filley property, presumably the same well from which Elsie had heard Albert pumping water. Albert's story of the crime offered no explanation for why the pistol was hidden there.

Searching for a clue as to the motive for the heinous crime, Sheriff Parker and the Caldwell County prosecutor returned to the Filley residence on Christmas Day to interview citizens of the neighborhood. One report said the two men "found a clew pointing to a close relationship between Filley and a woman who lived near," although the exact nature of the evidence was not stated. A separate report from near the same time said investigators had found a bureau drawer full of nice women's clothes belonging to Fannie Filley. Officers who'd investigated the murders and those who'd helped dress the victims for burial swore that no

such clothes were in the home on the day of the crime.
Perhaps this was part of the mysterious evidence suggesting
the involvement of another woman.

At his preliminary hearing on December 26, Filley
waived examination and was bound over to await the action
of the March term of circuit court. When his dead daughter,
Dolly, was mentioned, Filley reportedly trembled with
emotion, and tears came to his eyes.

In March 1908, Albert Filley's case was continued
until the June term of Caldwell County Circuit Court. About
the same time, Elsie Filley, who had previously brought a
civil suit against Albert for her husband's death, was awarded
damages of $1,000.

Albert Filley's first-degree murder trial for the death
of his wife finally got underway at Kingston on Monday,
June 22, before Judge F. H. Trimble. The courtroom was
"taxed to its capacity," according to one report, and it was
expected that attendance would only increase later in the
week after jury selection was complete.

Elsie Filley, the first witness called in the case, took
the stand on Wednesday afternoon in front of a packed
courtroom. She related essentially the same story she'd told
the coroner shortly after the crime, and the defendant broke
down and cried as she spoke.

The state's theory of the crime was that Filley had
tried to kill his wife a week before the murders, clubbing her
in the barn and falsely reporting that she'd been kicked by a
horse. When he realized that she was probably going to
recover from her injuries, he determined once again to kill
her.

The doctor who treated Fannie after the December 14
incident testified that her injuries were more consistent with
having been struck repeatedly with a board than with having
been kicked by a horse.

Asa Ecton, a neighbor who lived a quarter mile from
the Filley residence, said he saw Albert and Fannie go to the
barn on the 14th, saw Albert striking something or someone

with a club near the entrance to the barn, and heard a woman's voice cry, "Oh, don't!" He then saw Albert emerge from the barn alone and latch the door. After a delay of almost thirty minutes, Filley headed toward the J. W. Chaffin place.

Chaffin testified that, when Filley first summoned his help, he told him that his wife was dead from being kicked by a horse and asked Chaffin to go back and get Dolly for him. Filley was reluctant to return with Chaffin, but they soon went to the Filley barn together. Chaffin found the doors to the barn latched and the injured woman still lying in the stall with several horses standing calmly around her. Filley had made no attempt to remove her to safety. In addition, when Chaffin started to take the woman to the house, Filley showed no inclination to help, and Chaffin carried her by himself.

In the face of the overwhelming evidence against their client, Filley's lawyers chose to pursue an insanity defense. Several people who were related to Filley testified that mental illness ran in the family. Filley had one cousin in the insane asylum, the witnesses averred, and at least two other relatives who were subject to epileptic fits. The defense also called a medical expert who testified that, based on his examination of the defendant, he thought Filley was insane, while the state paraded its own expert to the stand as a rebuttal witness.

The case was given to the jury on Friday afternoon, June 26, and they deliberated for the next twenty-four hours with little time out for rest. On Saturday afternoon, the jury finally came back with a verdict finding Filley guilty of murder in the first degree and fixing his punishment at death. The jurors had agreed unanimously on the guilty verdict from the outset, but it took twenty-two ballots for them to agree on the death sentence. Filley reacted to the verdict with a slight tremor and a nervous movement of his hand, but his face showed no emotion.

Early the following week, Judge Trimble officially

pronounced the death sentence and set August 21 as the execution date. However, Filley's lawyers appealed to Missouri governor Joseph Folk for a commutation of sentence, and the governor granted a stay of execution until September 21 so that he could consider the matter. The delay met with widespread disapproval in the vicinity where the crimes were committed, and there was determined talk of mob action in case the governor ruled in Filley's favor.

On Friday, September 18, three days before Filley's scheduled execution, Governor Folk announced that he would not grant a commutation nor another reprieve. On the same day, Sheriff Parker asked Filley whether he wanted to see a spiritual advisor, and the prisoner replied that he did not. "If I did what they say I did," he explained, "I hope I'll burn forever."

TRIPLE MURDERER IS HANGED

Albert Filley Killed Wife, Brother and Baby Near Kingston.

KINGSTON, Mo., Sept. 21.—Albert Filley, the triple murderer, was hanged here at 6:02 this morning.

The *St. Louis Post-Dispatch* announces Filley's execution.

By Monday morning, though, Filley's defiant stoicism had softened in the face of imminent death, and he was accompanied to the gallows inside the county jail by a minister. Still, he ascended the scaffold without hesitation or a sign of fear and declined an offer to say any last words. His arms and legs were pinioned, the black cap was placed over his head, and the noose adjusted around his neck. It was 6:00 a.m. when the sheriff sprang the trap, and the condemned man shot through the opening before the gaping eyes of the twenty witnesses who'd been allowed inside the execution room. Filley was pronounced dead after fifteen minutes. His body was cut down, placed in a box, and sent to a local undertaker. The corpse was then turned over to relatives, who had Filley buried in McDaniel Cemetery beside the wife and child he'd killed.

25

A Dastardly Offense

The Lynching of Roy Hammonds

After Roy Hammonds, a young black man of nineteen, pled guilty on Friday, April 29, 1921, in the Circuit Court of Pike County, Missouri, to attempted assault on a fourteen-year-old white girl, he was assessed a sentence of ten years in the state penitentiary. But that wasn't enough for many of the good citizens around Bowling Green. They wanted him to hang.

Not just hang. They wanted him to suffer.

Two days earlier, Wednesday the 27th, fourteen-year-old Virginia Terrell had been to a picture show in Bowling Green and was walking home that night past the Negro Methodist Church in the southeast part of town when she was accosted by a black youth. Placing his hand over her mouth to keep her from screaming, the assailant dragged her to the rear of the church near a coal shed and started choking her, but the assault was interrupted by the girl's father and brother, who had started from their home to meet her. Hearing Virginia's screams, they came running, and the attacker fled at first sight of them.

The girl's father, H. J. Terrell, opened a pocket knife and dashed after the villain, causing the attacker to stumble and lose his cap as he jumped a fence. Regaining his footing, the young man fled through the town square of Bowling Green and past the jail, with Terrell, who'd been delayed crossing the fence, trailing behind him. Sheriff Charles P. Moore joined the chase, but the fugitive had "gained headway" by this time and eluded his pursuers.

Two bloodhounds were brought in from Moberly on

Thursday night, taken to the scene of the crime, and given the scent of the cap that the fugitive had lost. The dogs followed the path of the chase through the square, past the jail, and west on Locust Street, and then doubled back along a short line railroad to the home of Roy Hammonds north of Bowling Green. Several people were at the house, including Roy's father, William, and his older brother, Willie.

Based on the dogs' behavior and the fact that Virginia Terrell had described her attacker as a young black man, twenty-one-year-old Willie Hammonds was arrested and escorted to jail. The next morning, he was taken before the girl at the prosecutor's office in Bowling Green, and she identified him as the person who had attacked her. He was returned to the Pike County Jail over his stout protestations.

Shortly afterwards, Sheriff Moore tossed the cap found at the crime scene into Willie's cell, saying "Here's your cap."

"That's not my cap," Willie said. "That's Roy's cap."

William Hammonds, father of the two young men, confirmed that the cap belonged to Roy, but Roy claimed at first that Willie had been wearing it on the night of the attack. Confronted by his brother, he finally admitted that he had been wearing it. Both of the sons were then taken before the girl, and, after some deliberation, she picked out Roy as the one who had attacked her.

Roy then confessed his guilt and was tossed in jail. He admitted asking the girl to take off her clothes but she refused. That was all he did, he said, because the two men came up and he ran. His confession was reported as a written statement, but part of his statement was that he couldn't read and write. The confession was, in fact, transcribed by the prosecuting attorney, and parts of it were obviously prepared ahead of time, such as an assurance that the statement was made of Hammonds's "own volition" without coercion from either the prosecutor or the sheriff.

Roy's brother was released, but not before he cut his throat on a steel staple in his cell and almost bled to death.

Taken into court that same afternoon for a preliminary hearing, Roy pled guilty to assault, and Judge Edgar B. Woolfolk pronounced a sentence of ten years in the state penitentiary at Jefferson City.

Hundreds of people had flocked into Bowling Green from the countryside on Friday morning, as soon as a suspect was named in the attack on Virginia Terrell, and feelings against Hammonds ran high throughout the day. There were whisperings of vigilantism even before the preliminary hearing, and once the verdict was announced, talk of a lynching reached a fever pitch. Many in the community thought ten years in the can was not enough punishment for a black man who dared assault a young white girl.

Aware of the rumors of mob violence, Sheriff Moore decided to give the would-be vigilantes the slip. He put out the word that he planned to wait until Sunday to transfer Hammonds to the state prison when his real plan was to get the prisoner out of Bowling Green as soon as possible.

About dusk, Moore and six deputies took Hammonds by an indirect route to the Chicago and Alton Railroad station about a mile west of Bowling Green with the intention of boarding the 7:15 p.m. train for Mexico, Missouri, where they would make connections for Jefferson City. But somehow the lynch-happy crowd got wind of the ruse, and an undisguised and mostly unarmed mob began to form outside the depot before the westbound train showed up.

Moore placed his deputies outside as guards while he held the prisoner inside the building. A few minutes before the train's scheduled arrival, the vigilantes, now 200 strong, demanded that Hammonds be turned over to them, but the sheriff, speaking to the crowd through a window, refused. The deputies told the mob to disperse, but instead, when the whistle of the approaching train sounded in the distance, the lawless horde surged around the deputies and disarmed them.

When the train arrived, Moore pleaded with the crowd to respect the law and to let him board with his prisoner. "Bring him out and try it," one of the men shouted.

The train soon departed without the lawman and his prisoner, and as soon as it was gone, the vigilantes again demanded that the sheriff turn Hammonds over. When Moore refused, about six armed men broke into the office and mobbed him. The sheriff held his fire, saying later that he himself would have been killed if he had not done so, and the vigilantes quickly overpowered Moore and took his prisoner.

Hammonds, begging for his life, was placed in a car and taken west along the Curryville road to a tree about a mile distant from the railroad station, and a large procession of other automobiles followed. One man climbed the tree to fix a rope around a limb, and the other end was tied in a noose around Hammonds's neck.

The vengeful mob cruelly treated the young black man, purposely leaving his arms and legs unbound so that he would be "permitted to fight for his life" once he was dangling in the air. As the mob pulled him up, one of the lynchers yelled, "Take your time about dying."

Suspended almost ten feet from the ground, Hammonds reached above his head to grasp the rope and raise his body up to prevent strangulation. While in this position, he alternately prayed and begged for his life, as the vindictive crowd looked on in amusement. "He clung to the rope for fifteen minutes," said the *St. Louis Star and Tribune*, "and then, exhausted and realizing the fight was useless, gave up his efforts and was strangled."

After the mob was sure Hammonds was dead, they lowered his body and let a tramp passing by take the dead man's shoes and put them on his own feet.

On April 30, the day after the lynching, Pike County officials immediately began an investigation into the extralegal proceeding. Judge Woolfolk, prosecuting attorney Rufus Higginbotham, and the county coroner all vowed to do everything they could to bring the vigilantes to justice. Higginbotham appealed to the Missouri governor for assistance in the investigation, and the assistant attorney general for the state was assigned to the case.

Hammonds death certificate notes cause as hanging by parties unknown.
From the Missouri State Archives.

Sheriff Moore claimed not to recognize any of the mob, but one of his deputies said he recognized three of them. And a telegraph agent at the railroad station said he recognized the two men who stayed behind to guard the sheriff and his deputies after Hammonds was taken away.

A special session of the circuit court to investigate the lynching began on May 4 at Bowling Green. Instructing the grand jury there was no such thing as an "unwritten law," Judge Woolfolk called the lynching a "dastardly offense" and denounced the mob that took the law into its own hands.

Despite Woolfolk's stern charge to the jurors, they

came back on the afternoon of the next day, after interviewing about forty-five witnesses, and told the judge they had no indictments to present in the case. Although the lynchers were not masked, the witnesses claimed not to have recognized any of the vigilantes because of the darkness. Even those witnesses who had previously said they recognized some of the mob apparently had a sudden onset of amnesia. The Missouri assistant attorney general, who had been called in to aid the investigation, accused many of the witnesses of having perjured themselves to protect the mob, but the county prosecutor chose not to pursue the case further.

Typical Ozarks Hillbillies

The Hanging of the Lecherous Worden Brothers

During a single night in the fall of 1931, Elmer "Pete" Stevenson and brothers Lew and Harry Worden waylaid at least three carloads of people at gunpoint in Jasper County, Missouri, and raped three high school girls in the process.

But they paid a dear price for their criminal spree.

About eight o'clock on Sunday evening, November 15, 1931, twenty-year-old Norman Parks, eighteen-year-old George Mimms, and their fifteen-year-old girlfriends, Vera Hefley and Katherine Morris, were parked near the abandoned Coahuila mine about three and a half miles northwest of Carthage when a strange car pulled up beside them and stopped. Three men got out carrying revolvers and ordered the young people out of their automobile. Parks, who was behind the wheel, was struck on the head and shoulder when the order wasn't obeyed fast enough to suit the assailants.

One of the holdup men, later identified as thirty-one-year-old Pete Stevenson, escorted the two young men at gunpoint to the other side of a nearby chat pile, while his two accomplices, later identified as thirty-four-year-old Lew Worden and twenty-six-year-old Harry Worden, held the girls prisoner a short distance from the automobiles. The Worden brothers threatened to kill both girls if Vera didn't do as she was told. Lew then held the Morris girl at gunpoint while Harry escorted the Hefley girl into the nearby woods and sexually assaulted her.

After the attack, the three assailants took off in both

vehicles. Seeing no sign of Parks and Mimms, Vera and Katherine ran to a nearby farmhouse and frantically reported what had happened; the farmer helped the girls get back to Carthage. Vera was crying when she got home and had disheveled hair and soiled clothes. She immediately told her mother the awful news. The police were notified of the crime, and a physician was summoned to examine the girl.

Meanwhile, the highwaymen abandoned the Parks vehicle just south of Webb City. An hour and a half after the first attack, they held up a taxi cab near Carl Junction, about fifteen miles west of Carthage. Taking the cab driver and his two male and two female passengers to a wooded spot, they beat the driver about the head with a pistol and stole ten dollars each and some personal items from him and his two male passengers. The two young women were not molested.

Then, at ten p.m., the three desperadoes accosted another carload of young people near Peace Church Cemetery northwest of Joplin. The young victims were seventeen-year-old Arthur Poundstone, twenty-year-old Tom Wills, and their sixteen and seventeen-year-old female companions. All four were taken to an isolated spot west of the Jasper County Tuberculosis Hospital (near the present-day Joplin Regional Airport). This time Harry Worden guarded the young men while Lew Worden and Pete Stevenson raped the two girls. The villains then stole Poundstone's car and again drove away in two vehicles.

The holdups and assaults on November 15 were just the latest in a recent outbreak of attacks and highway robberies in the Jasper County area. Public outrage prompted an intense investigation, and suspicion quickly settled on the Worden brothers, who'd previously lived in Joplin, where Harry worked as a barber. During a police standoff with four road bandits a few years earlier, only one of the highwaymen was captured, and Harry Worden was suspected of being among the three who got away. He and his brother had been under police scrutiny ever since, but they had disappeared from Jasper County several months prior to the recent crimes.

A picture of Lew Worden was located, and the victims of the November 15 assaults near Carthage tentatively identified him as one of the men who'd perpetrated the outrage. The license number of the bandit car, as taken down by one of the victims, was matched to a tag stolen from an automobile near Birch Tree, Missouri, 170 miles east of Carthage, the previous July, and the Wordens were soon traced to nearby Mountain View. Lew Worden was taken into custody there on November 24, but local officers, under the impression that only Lew was wanted, allowed Harry Worden to escape.

Lew Worden was brought back to Carthage on November 25 and lodged in the Jasper County Jail. That evening he admitted his participation in the two holdups ten days earlier during which the three girls were sexually assaulted. He implicated his brother in the crimes but didn't know whether Harry or his other companion (whom he did not identify) had criminally assaulted any of the girls. He denied that he himself had raped any of them, admitting only that he had attempted to assault one of girls from the Poundstone vehicle but was unsuccessful. He explained that he and his companions had driven from Mountain View on the evening of the attacks, arriving shortly before the first assault, and that they'd returned to Mountain View in the wee hours of the following morning, abandoning Poundstone's automobile near Mountain View.

Brought to Joplin on the night of the 26th, Worden also confessed to the holdup of the taxi driver and his passengers. Poundstone, Wills, and their two young women companions viewed the suspect in the Joplin city jail and identified him as one of the men who had waylaid them. Charged with criminal assault on one of the girls, Worden was taken back to Carthage the next day and arraigned the day after that.

Harry Worden and Pete Stevenson were arrested in Illinois in early December after Stevenson got drunk and started bragging to two young women that he was a "bank bandit." Both men were returned to Missouri, but Stevenson, who'd still not been named as a suspect in the Jasper County assaults, was taken to Van Buren and held in the Carter County Jail on a robbery charge.

Worden, meanwhile, was brought to Carthage on December 7. When he was interrogated concerning the November 15 attacks on the young women, he admitted that he'd had sexual intercourse with one of the girls, but he denied that he'd used force.

Although both Wordens had pleaded not guilty at their initial appearances, Lew changed his tune when his trial came up in Division One of the Jasper County Circuit Court at Joplin on January 27, 1932. Throwing himself on the mercy of the court, he changed his plea to guilty, and his lawyers argued that his admission of guilt and the consequent sparing of the victim the ordeal of having to testify should warrant consideration for leniency. However, Judge Harvey Davis was in no mood to show mercy. "Any man who will go out on the highway and ravish a young girl deserves the death penalty," Davis declared in sentencing Worden to hang on March 3 at Carthage.

The next day, January 28, Harry Worden's trial began in Division Two before Judge Grant Emerson. The defense filed motions for a continuance, for a change of venue, and to have the jury panel quashed. In arguing the case for a change of venue, Worden's lawyers said the guilty plea in Lew Worden's case had prejudiced Jasper County citizens against their client, but Emerson denied all the defense motions. The rest of the day, and most of the next were spent in picking a jury.

Late on the afternoon of the 29th, Vera Hefley took the stand as the first state witness. She said she pleaded with Harry Worden to leave her alone but that he threatened to kill Katherine Morris, the best friend she had in the world, if she didn't do exactly what he told her to do. It was only then, fearing for her friend's life, that she quit trying to resist. Vera said that one of the Worden brothers also threatened, as they were leaving, to look her up if she said anything about what had happened. Katherine Morris and George Mimms followed Vera to the stand and confirmed her story in virtually every detail. (Norman Parks had taken a job in Detroit and moved away.)

Prosecution testimony continued the next morning, January 30, with Deputy Glenn Stemmons testifying that Harry Worden had confessed to criminal assault shortly after being brought back to Carthage. Harry Worden's lawyers then presented their case the same day. The main defense witness was Worden's wife, Blanche, who testified to her husband's lack of education and dull-wittedness.

The case went to the jury in the late afternoon, and they came back that evening with a guilty verdict after deliberating about three hours. A unanimous jury vote fixed the penalty at death, and the judge formally pronounced the sentence on February 1. The verdict was quickly appealed to the Missouri Supreme Court, however, and the execution date indefinitely postponed.

After several weeks of negotiations between Jasper County and Carter County officials, Pete Stevenson was finally brought to Carthage on February 18, lodged in the Jasper County Jail, and charged as the third assailant in the November 15 assaults.

Meanwhile, Lew Worden's lawyers appealed to the Missouri governor to commute their client's sentence to life imprisonment or at least grant a stay of execution until after Harry Worden's case was settled. They argued that it was grossly unfair to execute a man who had pled guilty to an offense before executing a partner in crime who had pled not guilty to the same offense. Stanley Clay, Lew's lead lawyer, described his client as a "typical Ozarks hillbilly" and "a moron" who was incapable of understanding why he should be hanged for what he had done. The governor, however, declined to intervene in the case, declaring that it should not be a foregone conclusion that a person could escape the death penalty just by pleading guilty.

Joplin Police mug shot of Lew Worden. *Courtesy Jasper County Records Center.*

As Lew Worden's execution day approached, family members, including his mother, visited him in his cell at the Carthage jail, and Lew helped make his own funeral arrangements. As an honorably discharged veteran of World War I, he was accorded military rites, although the local American Legion declined to participate in the planned service. Worden, who'd recently professed religion, blamed his troubles on "whiskey and sin."

On the early morning of March 3, 1932, Lew Worden walked calmly to the gallows erected just outside the county jail at Carthage. About 100 observers, including the father of the girl Worden attacked, were allowed inside the stockade surrounding the gallows, while a crowd of about 500 thronged around the enclosure. After the preparations were made, Worden dropped through the trap at 6:02 a.m. and was pronounced dead twelve minutes later. A Carthage funeral home took charge of the body, services were held in Joplin a couple of days later, and Worden was buried in Joplin's Forest Park Cemetery.

Coverage of the Worden case had been the lead

headline in recent editions of the local newspapers, but Lew's execution was relegated to a subhead by the kidnapping of the Lindbergh baby.

At the April term of Jasper County Circuit Court, Pete Stevenson was granted a change of venue to neighboring Lawrence County. He pled guilty there on Monday, May 23, was sentenced to ninety-nine years in the state penitentiary, and was taken to Jefferson City later in the week.

On December 14, 1932, the Missouri Supreme Court affirmed the lower court's decision in Harry Worden's case and reset his execution for January 20, 1933. Worden's lawyers then appealed to newly elected governor Guy B. Park for clemency, and a number of people from Jasper County wrote letters supporting the appeal. Harry's wife traveled to Jefferson City to present the governor with several of the letters. On January 18, less than forty-eight hours before Worden was scheduled to die, Park issued a stay of execution until February 10, announcing that he needed more time to study the case.

As the February 10 deadline approached, Worden's lawyers renewed their appeal to the governor asking that he commute their client's sentence to life imprisonment, but this time Park declined to interfere. Worden was put on a death watch, and he was visited regularly by his wife and his spiritual advisor, the Rev. Dow Booe, a Pentecostal preacher who had also been Lew Worden's minister during his final days. On the evening of February 9, Harry issued a public statement, confessing to the crime he'd been convicted of and asking for God's mercy.

On the early morning of February 10, Harry Worden, like his brother before him, marched to the gallows with outward calm. After he stepped on the trap and the noose was adjusted around his neck, he bid the sheriff goodbye but made no further statement. The trap was sprung at 5:59 a.m., and Worden was pronounced dead after twelve minutes. The execution took place inside the jail building in a room on the second floor with about fifty witnesses in attendance. It was

the same room from which Lew Worden had begun his death
march to an outside scaffold forty-nine weeks earlier.

Harry Worden Is Hanged For Attack on a School Girl

Former Joplin Barber Goes to Gallows Calmly at Carthage Jail.

Headline proclaims Harry Worden's fate. From the *Maryville Daily Forum*.

Harry Worden's body was taken to a funeral home in
Galena, Kansas, Rev. Booe's hometown. He was interred in
Galena's Hill Crest Cemetery.

At the time of Worden's execution, a Carter County
newspaper lamented the fact that Pete Stevenson, despite
being "generally regarded as the leader of the gang," had
escaped the death sentence. But his reprieve didn't last long.
He died in prison at Jefferson City in May of 1934.

Bibliographical Notes

Chapter 1 (An Unnatural and Atrocious Crime). My main sources for this chapter were the *St. Louis Missouri Gazette and Public Advertiser*, January 10 and May 9, 1821; and the *History of Southeast Missouri*.

Chapter 2 (An Election Day Mob). The principal sources for this chapter were Shetley, *Historical Madison*; *History of Southeast Missouri*; *St. Louis Daily Missouri Republican*, 12 August 1844; *New York Herald*, 16 October 1844; and Letter from daughter of Thomas Vincent, 15 January 1900, http://wc.rootsweb.ancestry.com/cgi-bin/igm.cgi?op=GET&db=grantpinnix&id=I050999.

Chapter 3 (A Terrible Murder). Important sources for this chapter were *History of Gentry and Worth Counties, Missouri*; *Meigs County (OH) Telegraph*, 7 September 1858, quoting the *St. Louis Republican*; *Memphis Daily Appeal*, 16 July 1858, quoting the *St. Joseph Gazette*; *Richmond Dispatch*, 8 July 1858, quoting the *St. Louis Republican*; and *Baltimore Daily Exchange*, 9 July 1858, quoting the *St. Louis News* and 12 July 1858, quoting the *St. Joseph Journal*.

Chapter 4 (The Public Strangling of a Criminal). Governors Papers, Missouri State Archives; *History of Laclede, Camden, Dallas, Webster...*; *Fayetteville (TN) Observer*, 25 April 1872, quoting the *Marshfield Citizen*; *Springfield Leader*, 23 May 1872 and 8 February 1877; and *New York Times*, 3 September 1870, quoting the *Chicago Tribune*, were among important sources consulted for this chapter.

Chapter 5 (The Depraved Condition of Society). Important sources for this chapter included the *Sedalia Bazoo*, 31 August 1880 and 26 July 1881; *Sedalia Democratic Press*, 10

December 1868; *Lincoln County (MO) Herald*, 10 December 1868; Oregon *Holt County Sentinel*, 2 April 1869; *Bloomington (IL) Pantagraph*, 23 August 1880; *St. Louis Post Dispatch*, 22 July 1881; and the *History of Henry and St. Clair Counties*.

Chapter 6 (Taken Up). "History of Washington County Missouri Jails;" *New York Herald*, 28 January 1871; *Richmond (VA) Daily Dispatch*, 3 December 1870, quoting the *Washington County (MO) Journal*; *Troy Lincoln County (MO) Herald*, 2 February 1871, quoting the *St. Louis Democrat*; *New Orleans Republican*, 25 November 1870; and the *History of Franklin, Jefferson, Washington…* were among the principal sources for this chapter.

Chapter 7 (Dead! Dead! Dead!) My main references for this chapter were the *Osceola Democrat*, 8 and 15 July 1871; the *Osceola Herald*, 6, 13, and 29 July 1871; and the *History of Henry and St. Clair Counties*.

Chapter 8 (Bill Young's Busy Week). Important sources for this chapter were the *History of Lewis, Clark, Knox and Scotland Counties*; *Shelbyville (MO) Shelby County Herald*, 9 June 1880, quoting *LaGrange (MO) Democrat* and August 15, 1877, quoting the *St. Louis Globe-Democrat; Mexico Weekly Ledger*, 17 June 1880; *Shelbina (MO) Democrat*, 5 November 1879, quoting the *Keokuk (IA) Gate City*; *Des Moines Register*, 31 October 1879, quoting the *Keokuk Gate City*; and *Burlington Weekly Hawkeye*, 3 November 1860, quoting the *Alexandria (MO) Delta*.

Chapter 9 (A Demoniac Case). The *St. Louis Post-Dispatch*, 15 and 21 August 1879, 14 June 1880, 20, 24, and 27 November 1880, 25 October 1881, 11, 12, and 13 January 1882, was the primary source for this chapter. Other newspapers consulted include the *Somerset (PA) Herald*, 20 August 1879; *Chicago Tribune*, 17 August 1879; and *New*

York Times, 14 January 1882.

Chapter 10 (What I Have Done Deserves Death). Important references for this chapter were *Reports of Cases Argued and Determined in the Supreme Court of the State of Missouri*, v. 97; *History of Andrew and DeKalb Counties; Oregon Holt County Sentinel*, 5 and 12 September 1884; *St. Joseph Gazette*, 4 September 1884; and *Sedalia Weekly Bazoo*, 25 November 1884.

Chapter 11 (A Red-Handed Desperado). The following newspapers were primary sources for this chapter: *Maryville Nodaway Democrat*, 6 March 1879; *St. Louis Post-Dispatch*, 9 and 15 December 1884; *St. Joseph Gazette-Herald*, 10 December 1884; and *St. Joseph Weekly Herald*, 11 and 18 December 1884.

Chapter 12 (The Damned Thing Has Got to Be Rid Of). *The Butler Weekly Times*, 23 January 1889 and 6 July 1893; *Chillicothe Morning Constitution*, 30 April 1891; *Kansas City Gazette*, 27 July 1889; *Keytesville Chariton Courier*, 10 April and 18 December 1890, 15 October 1891, and 5 November 1891; *Leavenworth (KS) Times*, 27 July 1889; *Macon Times*, 25 January 1889 and 16 October 1891; *Pittsburg (KS) Headlight*, 1 August 1889; *St. Joseph Weekly Herald*, 1 August 1889, 5 November 1891, and 29 June and 10 August 1893; and *Trenton Evening Republican*, 3 and 4 August 1893; were among the newspapers consulted for this chapter. Other sources include *Reports of Cases Argued and Determined in the Supreme Court of the State of Missouri*, vols. 100 and 117 and the *Southwest Reporter*, vol. 31.

Chapter 13 (A Professional Butcher Slaughters His Own Family), Among the newspapers consulted for this chapter were the *Kansas City Journal*, 10, 11, and 15 June, 6 and 14 July, and 10 October 1897; *St. Louis Post-Dispatch*, 25 April 1891 and 30 March 1899; *St. Joseph Weekly Gazette*, 1 April

1880 and 30 April 1891; *Salem (OR) Statesman Journal*, 12 June 1897; *Sedalia Weekly Democrat*, 19 and 31 March and 7 April 1899; and *Springfield Leader-Democrat*, 30 November 1897. Other important sources include Webber, *History and Directory of Cass County* and the *Southwestern Reporter*, v. 49.

Chapter 14 (Bald Knobberism Revived). Important sources for this chapter include Hartman and Ingenthron, *Bald Knobbers*; the *Butler Weekly Times*, 1 June and 17 July 1892; Haworth, "Taney County Bald Knobbers;" Mahnkey, "The George L. Williams Memorial Library;" *Springfield Daily Democrat*, 15 March 1892; and *Springfield Leader, 11, 12, 14, and 15 March 1892.*

Chapter 15 (A Prussian General Dies on the Gallows). My main source for this chapter was the *St. Louis Post-Dispatch*. I consulted many issues, including 14, 15, 18, 19, 21, 26, and 27 February 1894; 1 March and 16 September 1894; 22 January and 12 August 1895; and 19 January and 16 February 1897. T*he Southwestern Reporter*, v. 38, was also a vital source. Other sources consulted include the *Butler Weekly Times*, 22 August 1895, citing the *St. Louis Globe-Democrat*, and the *Union Tribune-Republican*, 17 January 1896.

Chapter 16 (They'll Make Me Die Hard). Main sources for this chapter were the *Kansas City Journal*, 31 July 1895; *Mexico Weekly Ledger*, 25 July 1895, quoting the *Fulton Telegraph*, and 22 August 1895, quoting the *Auxvasse Review*; *Sedalia Weekly Democrat*, 2 and 15 August 1895.

Chapter 17 (A Record for Speedy Justice). The main sources for this chapter were the *Southwestern Reporter*, v. 37; *Springfield Leader-Democrat*, 25 May 1896; *Springfield Republican*, 26 May 1896 and 31 January 1897; *Taney County Republican*, 28 May 1896, 4 June 1896, and 29 October 1896; and Curry, *A Reminiscent History of Douglas County*.

Chapter 18 (Deliberately Planned and Skillfully Executed). *Pacific Transcript*, 9 and 16 July 1897; *St. Louis Post-Dispatch*, 4, 5, 10, and 11 July and 21 September 1897; and *Union Franklin County Tribune*, 9 and 16 July and 1 October 1897; were the main sources for this chapter.

Chapter 19 (Kissin' Cousin Turned Killin' Cousin). The *Southwestern Reporter*, v. 56, was an important reference for this chapter. These newspapers also provided essential information: The *Kansas City Journal*, 10, 13, and 14 December 1898, 7, 8, 18, and 21 April 1898, and 22 November 1899; *Kansas City Star*, 9 December 1898; *King City Chronicle*, 21 April 1899; *St. Joseph Gazette-Herald*, 9 and 10 December 1898, 21 April and 8 November 1899, 6 January, 26 May and 15 June 1900; *St. Joseph Herald*, 18 December 1898 and 22 November 1899; *St. Louis Post-Dispatch*, 10 and 11 December 1898, 8 May and 15 June 1900; and *Sedalia Democrat*, 9 December 1898 and 9 November 1899.

Chapter 20 (The Savage Instinct to Kill). The main sources for this chapter were the *Marshall Republican*, 6 April and 4 May 1900; and *St. Louis Republic*, 2 May 1900, quoting the *Marshall Democrat News*.

Chapter 21 (Daring to Curse a White Boy). The main sources for this chapter were the *St. Louis Republic*, 18 February 1902; *Indianapolis Freeman*, 15 March 1902; *New Madrid Weekly Record*, 22 February 1902; and *New Madrid Southeast Missourian*, 20 February 1902. Other newspapers consulted include the *Coffeyville (KS) Weekly Journal*, 21 February 1902; *Independence (KS) Daily Reporter*, 19 February 1902; *Belvidere (IL) Daily Republican*, 18 February 1902; and *St. Paul Globe*, 17 March 1902.

Chapter 22 (Too Many Wives). For this chapter, I consulted, among other sources, the *Caruthersville Pemiscot Press*, 30 April, 7 May, and 21 May 1903; *Caruthersville Twice-A-*

Week Democrat, 1 and 5 May 1903; *Hayti Herald*, 13 October 1910, citing the *New Madrid Southeast Missourian*; *St. Louis Republic*, 4, 7 and 8 May 1903; and *Reports of Cases Determined Before the Supreme Court of the State of Missouri*, v. 191.

Chapter 23 (Would Have Done a White Man the Same Way). The main sources for this chapter were the *Benton Scott County Kicker*, 20 May 1905; *Charleston Courier*, 19 May 1905; *Chillicothe Constitution-Tribune*, 13 May 1905; *Guthrie Oklahoma Safeguard*, 18 May 1905; *Jackson Herald*, 25 May 1905; *Los Angeles Herald*, 21 May 1905; and *St. Louis Republic*, 17 May 1905.

Chapter 24 (I Hope I Burn Forever). The *Chillicothe Constitution-Tribune*, numerous dates, including 24 and 27 December 1907; 11, 25, 26, 27, and 29 June 1908; 18 August, 19 September, and 21 September 1908; was the main source for this chapter. I also consulted the S*edalia Democrat*, 22 June 1907, and "Henry Clay Filley's Story of His Death."

Chapter 25 (A Dastardly Offense). The main source for this chapter was the *Bowling Green Times*, 5 May 1921. Other newspapers consulted include the *Columbia Evening Missourian*, 30 April, 3 May, and 4 May 1921; *Kansas City Times*, 30 April 1921; *Macon Chronicle-Herald*, 16 August 1921; *St. Louis Post-Dispatch*, 6 and 7 May 1921; and *St. Louis Star and Tribune*, 30 April 1921.

Chapter 26 (Typical Ozarks Hillbillies). The main sources for this chapter were Duncan, *Notorious*; Worden newspaper clippings at Jasper County Records Center; *Jefferson City Post-Tribune*, 23 February 1932; and *Joplin Globe*, numerous dates, including especially 17 and 27 November 1931, 28, 30, and 31 January 1932, 1 and 3 March 1932, and 11 February 1933.

Bibliography

Books

Curry, J. E. *A Reminiscent History of Douglas County, Missouri, 1857-1957*. Ava: Douglas County Herald, 1957.

Duncan, Barry. *Notorious: The Gangster Era in Carthage and Jasper County, Missouri*. The Author, 2015.

Hartman, Mary and Elmo Ingenthron. *Bald Knobbers: Vigilantes on the Ozarks Frontier*. Gretana (LA): Pelican Publishing Company, 1989.

History of Andrew and DeKalb Counties, Missouri. Chicago: Goodspeed Publishing Co., 1888.

History of Franklin, Jefferson, Washington Crawford and Gasconade Counties, Missouri. Chicago: Goodspeed Publishing Co., 1888.

History of Gentry and Worth Counties, Missouri. St. Joseph: National Historical Company, 1882.

History of Henry and St. Clair Counties, Missouri. St. Joseph: National Historical Company, 1883

History of Laclede, Camden, Dallas, Webster, Wright, Texas, Pulaski, Phelps and Dent Counties, Missouri. Chicago: Goodspeed Publishing Company, 1889.

History of Lewis, Clark, Knox and Scotland Counties, Missouri. St. Louis: Goodspeed Publishing Co., 1887.

History of Southeast Missouri, Embracing an Historical Account of the Counties of Ste. Genevieve, St. Francois, Perry, Cape Girardeau, Bollinger, Madison, New Madrid, Pemiscot, Dunklin, Scott, Mississippi, Stoddard, Butler and Iron. Chicago: Goodspeed Publishing Co., 1888.

Reports of Cases Argued and Determined in the Supreme Court of the State of Missouri. F. M. Brown, reporter. v. 97. Columbia (MO): E.W. Stephens, 1889.

_____F. M. Brown, reporter. v. 100, Columbia: E.W.

Stephens, 1890.
_____F. M. Brown, reporter. v. 117, Columbia: E.W. Stephens, 1894.

Reports of Cases Determined in the Supreme Court of the State of Missouri, Between November 21 and December 12, 1905. v. 191. Perry S. Rader, Reporter. Columbia: E.W. Stephens, 1906.

Shetley, Paula. *Historical Madison: the History of Madison County, Missouri, 1818-1988.* Fredericktown (MO): Madison County Historical Society, 1989.

Southwestern Reporter, v. 31, June 10-July 29, 1895. St. Paul: West Publishing Co., 1895.

_____, v. 37, October 19, 1896-January 4, 1897. St. Paul: West Publishing Co., 1897.

_____, v. 38, January 11-March 8, 1897. St. Paul: West Publishing Co., 1897

_____, v. 49, February 13-April 3, 1899. St. Paul: West Publishing Co., 1899.

_____, v. 56, April 23-June 11, 1900. St. Paul: West Publishing Co., 1900.

Webber, A. L. *History and Directory of Cass County, Missouri.* Harrisonville: The Cass County Leader, 1908

Unpublished Documents and Government Records

Birth and Death Certificates database, Missouri State Archives, Jefferson City. https://s1.sos.mo.gov/records/archivesdb/birthdeath/.

Governors Records, Benjamin Gratz Brown Collection, Missouri State Archives, Jefferson City. http://www.sos.mo.gov/archives/mdh_splash/default.asp?coll=brown.

Penitentiary Records, Missouri State Archives, Jefferson City. https://s1.sos.mo.gov/records/archives/archivesdb/msp/.

Indiana Marriages, www.familysearch.org.

Missouri Marriages, www.familysearch.org.
U.S. Census Records, www.familysearch.org.
Worden newspaper clippings at Jasper County Records
    Center, Carthage.
Worth County Circuit Court Records.

Print and Online Articles

Haworth, I. J. "Taney County Bald Knobbers," *White River
    Valley Historical Quarterly*, v. 9, no. 3 (Spring 1986).
"Henry   Clay   Filley's   Story   of   His   Death,"
    https://familysearch.org/photos/artifacts/2705010.
History   of   Washington   County   Missouri   Jails.
    http://carrollscorner.net/SitesWashCo_Jails.htm.
Letter from daughter of Thomas Vincent, 15 January 1900.
    http://wc.rootsweb.ancestry.com/cgi-bin/igm.cgi?
    op=GET&db=grantpinnix&id=I050999.
Mahnkey, Douglas, "The George L. Williams Memorial
    Library," *White River Valley Historical Quarterly*, v.
    5, no. 6 (Winter 1974-1975) and v. 5, no. 10 (Winter
    1975-1976).

Newspapers

Belvidere (IL) Daily Republican.
Baltimore Daily Exchange.
Benton Scott County Kicker.
Bloomington (IL) Pantagraph.
Bowling Green Times.
Burlington Weekly Hawkeye.
Butler Weekly Times.
Cape Girardeau Democrat.
Caruthersville Twice-A-Week Democrat.
Caruthersville Pemiscot Press.
Charleston Courier.
Chicago Tribune.
Chillicothe Constitution-Tribune.

Chillicothe Morning Constitution.
Coffeyville (KS) Weekly Journal.
Columbia Evening Missourian.
Des Moines Register.
Fayetteville (TN) Observer.
Forsyth Taney County Republican.
Guthrie Oklahoma Safeguard.
Hayti Herald.
Independence (KS) Daily Reporter.
Indianapolis Freeman.
Jackson Herald.
Jefferson City State Republican.
Kansas City Gazette.
Kansas City Journal.
Kansas City Star.
Kansas City Times.
Keytesville Chariton Courier.
King City Chronicle.
Leavenworth (KS) Times.
Los Angeles Herald.
Macon Chronicle-Herald.
Macon Times.
Marshall Republican.
Maryville Nodaway Democrat.
Meigs County (OH) Telegraph.
Memphis Daily Appeal.
Mexico Weekly Ledger.
New Madrid Southeast Missourian.
New Madrid Weekly Record.
New Orleans Republican.
New York Herald.
New York Times.
Oregon Holt County Sentinel.
Osceola Democrat.
Osceola Herald.
Pacific Transcript.
Pittsburg (KS) Headlight.

Richmond (VA) Dispatch.
St. Joseph Gazette.
St. Joseph Gazette-Herald.
St. Joseph Herald.
St. Joseph Weekly Herald.
St. Louis Daily Missouri Republican.
St. Louis Missouri Gazette and Public Advertiser.
St. Louis Post-Dispatch.
St. Louis Republic.
St. Louis Star and Tribune.
St. Paul Globe.
Salem (OR) Statesman Journal.
Sedalia Democrat.
Sedalia Democratic Press.
Sedalia Weekly Bazoo.
Sedalia Weekly Democrat.
Shelbina Democrat.
Shelbyville Shelby County Herald.
Somerset (PA) Herald.
Springfield Daily Democrat.
Springfield Leader.
Springfield Leader-Democrat.
Springfield Missouri Weekly Patriot.
Springfield Republican.
Trenton Evening Republican.
Troy Lincoln County Herald.
Union Franklin County Tribune.
Union Tribune-Republican.

Index

Booe, Dow, 202, 203
Booher, Charlie, 71, 72, 73, 77
Bourbeuse River, 145
Bowling Green, Missouri, 122, 123, 190, 191, 192, 194
Bray, Lydia, 56, 59, 61
Bridges, J. H., 137
Bright, John Wesley, 103, 104, 105, 106, 107, 108, 110, 111
Bright, Matilda, 103, 105, 107, 108
Broadus, E. J., 152
Brookfield, Missouri, 86, 87, 89, 90, 91, 92
Brooks, A. J., 94
Brooks, Sarah, 89
Brown, Agnes, 143, 146
Brown, Erastus "Ras", 139, 140, 142, 143, 144, 145
Brown, Frank, 143, 146
Brown, Gratz, 27, 28, 30
Brown, Julia, 139, 142, 143, 145, 146
Brown, Thomas, 49, 50
Brown, Walter, 56, 57
Brownington, Missouri, 33, 34
Buchanan, John, 124, 125
Buckner, Ed, 124, 125
Cain, Jennie, 121, 122, 123, 124
Cain, John W., 121, 122
Caldwell County Circuit Court, 186
Calwood, Missouri, 124, 125
Cameron, Missouri, 182, 183
Cantrell Creek, 25
Cape Girardeau County Jail, 15
Carl Junction, Missouri, 197
Carlock, Henry, 19
Carter County Jail, 199
Carthage, Missouri, 34, 35, 36, 196, 197, 198, 199, 200, 201
Caruthers, David L., 8, 9, 10, 11, 13
Caruthersville, Missouri, 168, 169, 170, 171, 172
Cass County Jail, 98
Chaffin, J. W., 182, 183, 184, 187

About the Author

Larry Wood is a retired public school teacher and freelance writer specializing in the history of Missouri and the Ozarks. He has published fourteen books on regional history and two historical novels. His numerous stories and articles have appeared in magazines and journals ranging from the *Missouri Historical Review* to *Wild West Magazine*. An honorary lifetime member of the Missouri Writers' Guild, Wood maintains a blog on Ozarks history at www.ozarks-history.blogspot.com and writes a weekly newspaper column on Missouri and Ozarks history. He and his wife, Gigi, live in Joplin, Missouri.